The Curriculum Bridge

The Curriculum Bridge

From Standards to Actual Classroom Practice

Pearl G. Solomon

CORWIN PRESS, INC.
A Sage Publications Company
Thousand Oaks, California

For information:

Corwin Press, Inc.
A Sage Publications Company
2455 Teller Road
Thousand Oaks, California 91320
E-mail: order@corwinpress.com

SAGE Publications Ltd.
6 Bonhill Street
London EC2A 4PU
United Kingdom

SAGE Publications India Pvt. Ltd.
M-32 Market
Greater Kailash I
New Delhi 110 048 India

Printed in the United States of America

Library of Congress Cataloging-in-Publication Data

Solomon, Pearl G. (Pearl Gold), 1929–
  The curriculum bridge: From standards to actual classroom
practice / Pearl G. Solomon.
    p. cm.
  Includes bibliographical references and index.
  ISBN 0-8039-6704-7 (cloth: acid-free paper)
  ISBN 0-8039-6705-5 (pbk.: acid-free paper)
  1. Curriculum planning—United States.
  2. Education—Curricula—Standards—United States.
  3. Educational tests and measurements.
  4. Curriculum-based assessment—United States. I. Title.
LB2806.15 .S65   1998
375′.001—ddc21
                                          98-8896
This book is printed on acid-free paper.

98 99 00 01 02 03 04 7 6 5 4 3 2 1

Production Editor: Sherrise M. Purdum
Production Assistant: Karen Wiley
Editorial Assistant: Kristen L. Gibson
Typesetter/Designer: Christina M. Hill
Cover Designer: Marcia M. Rosenburg
Print Buyer: Anna Chin

Contents

Preface

Who Should Read This Book

Good investments provide us with profitable returns. Money and time are the currencies of investments in the process of education, investments whose purpose is to protect our futures and that of society. This book is for those of us who want to make an investment of time that may help us understand how to make better decisions about what students should and can learn and how we can help them learn. It explains why there is growing mistrust of the return on the investment in education in this country, why there is a cry for new higher standards and accountability. It will prepare us to make a knowing and credible response to those who have a lack of faith in what we do. The time spent should give us greater confidence in our ability to identify the problems and find the solutions for whatever others have found deficient or convince them to judge otherwise. My own investment of time in preparation for this book was made because I am a teacher and know that learning and writing about what I need to do will help me become a better one.

Profitable returns on investments require more than superficial suggestions. Although a basic philosophy about what is right in curriculum is embedded in this book, it is not a philosophical treatise. It is more of an informed "how to do it." Unlike other curriculum books it deals mostly with the present and with current needs. It does not address the specific content of differnt subject areas; instead it provides an overall view that can help educators and otehr educational decision makers as they respond to the needs fo their students and the demands of policy-makers for higher standards. Although theres is a strong emphasis on the research knowl-edge that should guide us in building curriculum, the book is not a com-prehensive review of the literature. It does try to synthesize and represent the thoughts of many current researchers in a manner that can easily be understood and applied to classroom practice. Therefore, those who prac-tice and those who lead others in their proctice may benefit from the chap-ters ahead.

What This Book Is About

This book is about curriculum and the skeleton that gives it a frame and support: the standards or levels of the bar that represent what we value, what we know and what our children need to know. A shared understanding of the meaning of curriculum and classroom practice is a good way to begin. A variety of people and institutions make educational decisions, but for professional educators, it is their major endeavor and responsibility. They make long-term decisions that affect many students and small ones that are momentary, aimed at one particular student in a specific instance. The set of school-based decisions about what and how children should learn is the *curriculum.*

Regardless of whether curriculum decisions are made by an individual teacher or a consensus of teachers, or imposed as a policy by those in authority, if they are planned and documented, they constitute the *written curriculum.* Not everything is written down, and not everything written is accomplished. The planned and unplanned decisions made and the ac-tions taken by teachers in classrooms (with the written curriculum and other things in mind) are referred to as the *enacted curriculum,* which is in essence, classroom practice. The unwritten curriculum is sometimes referred to as the *hidden curriculum,* but it is not hidden from classroom practice.

Embedded in the chapters ahead is a real story of three teachers as they confront the current issues that concern schools and discover what is now known about learning. Based on this new knowledge, they work together to pursue some specific strategies that will help them use the standards skeleton to build the curriculum bridge to classroom practice. And then they will look at the future. Their task will not be easy.

When educators are given the authority to enact curriculum, they have power—more than they probably realize. However, when parents and the public-at-large entrust teachers with this power over their chil-dren, they retain some rights to monitor and control what teachers do. Teachers then juggle constantly. In one hand are the balls that represent what they believe is best for that child and themselves, at this time, in this place. These beliefs are based on their standards, their values, their interests, their knowledge of the content of the curriculum, their knowledge of their own skills, and their knowledge of their students. In the other hand is their obligation to respect the beliefs of others who have a stake in students' futures: parents, supervisors, elected officials, and the public-at-large.

The juggling act is tricky. It demands concentration and practice. Teachers must know where each ball is at all times. Because they must respond to different students at different moments in time, they need to reflectively monitor their own beliefs. They need to listen carefully to the voices of others who influence what they are doing, and be alert to a lack of fit. Sometimes adjustments will be necessary, but at other times their beliefs should be held firm. The rhythm, balance, and consistency are important. Skill with old moves increases with experience, but new moves make performance better and more interesting.

In Chapter 1, "Weren't There Always Curriculum Standards?" readers will discover or be reminded of some of the recent history that has brought us to the current crescendo of public interest in education and the trend toward the adoption of a common core of high standards for student achievement. The present is viewed through the comments of the public, respected educational leaders, and politicians in regard to the current status of education. They are worthy of the attention because it is important to understand the influences and controls that affect our values, effectiveness, and choices.

Chapter 2, "Are New Standards Necessary?" explores these influences. Influences may not have clearly definable consequences when you do not pay attention to them. But if we are teachers, their power is related to our own needs. Our strongest imperative is to reach our students—and we struggle to do the best we can. Controls, such as high-stakes tests based on imposed standards, can have clearly definable consequences for students and for ourselves. The cogent strategy is to make the influences and controls of a variety of stakeholders work for our purposes rather than against them.

Chapter 2 will help us gain an understanding of the underlying struggle in this country for control of public education. Beginning with the politically charged debate between federal and state governments over who should determine standards, it considers the role of the press and big business in framing the dimensions of the discourse. It then moves to the role of local school boards and their relationship with the internal power system of supervision by school administrators and the unpredictable power of parents. Included among the other influences addressed are the subtle pressures of peers and professional peer groups, college professors, and professional writers, and, because education is a major enterprise, the powerful lure of an abundance of commercial materials and new technologies.

Chapter 3, "What We Now Know About How Learning Happens," brings us to the heart of the enacted curriculum with an abbreviated discussion of what we now know about learning. The briefing on the knowledge base is intended to provide us with a rationale or decision-making template for the curriculum content and instructional strategies that we classroom teachers may choose. It will help us predict more cogently what will work and understand why some things do not work. It is in this knowledge that true power lies. The best use of that power includes a reflective process that is progenerative, leading us continuously to self-correction and renewal. This chapter ends with a summary analysis that applies current knowledge of how learning takes place to specific suggestions for curriculum and instructional practice.

Chapter 4, "Choosing Standards and Designing Them Down," will take us to the creative design step: constructing our own curriculum. Once all of the influences, controls, and existing sources have been considered, the teacher is ready to identify what standards students must meet and which additional outcomes are desired (the desired outcomes may exceed the standards). This chapter will provide clarification of the new terminology and compare it to the existing terms and habits of practice so that we may all speak the same new language. It will offer a template to guide us as we design down from more general prescribed national or state standards to the specific outcomes we aim for with an individual classroom experience.

It is a challenge to match desired outcomes with appropriate learning experiences for students, experiences in settings that reflect the many new understandings that we now have about how learning happens and about what keeps it from happening. Before writing this book, for example, I thought about the outcomes I wished to achieve, but knowing how learning takes place humbled my expectations for accomplishing them with just a reading activity. However, that same knowledge about learning has made me rethink the way in which this reading activity is organized. Using a metaphor of the theater, Chapter 5, "Constructing Creative Classrooms," takes us through the setting parameters of grouping students, using time, space, and material props. It addresses the role of student goals in motivating and managing learning, and then explores the use of critical themes and classroom discourse.

Unfortunately, a missing element in this educational activity is my ability to assess its effect on my readers. Assessments produce the signals for our educational transport system that takes students from the place of not knowing to knowing. We teacher-engineers need to know where we are going, how well and how fast we are progressing, where the switches are, and if the track is obstructed, what the alternative routes are. We also need to stop at a station from time to time to refuel, revise, and take on new passengers and new systems. Assessments guide our station breaks.

Chapter 6, "How Are We Doing? Measuring Success," compares how traditional and alternative assessments are used to tell how our students and therefore we, ourselves are doing with chosen purposes. Well done assessments can be designed to discover previously unrevealed positive outcomes and undiscovered needs. They can also be used to enforce curriculum policy mandates. Performance assessments will be explored as an alternative or addition to short answer tests of recall of finite and unrevealing facts, measured by percentages of correct responses for predetermined answers. These measure a wider scope of newly constructed knowledge and use open-ended problems that allow for divergent solutions. This chapter looks at rubrics that identify more clearly what has or hasn't been accomplished, and do it in a way that can provide better direction for new learning activities.

Chapter 7, "Where Do We Go From Here?" looks at ways to increase the potential return on investments. Ensuring a good return requires learning new skills and sharing skills with others in a meaningful way. It examines the possible reasons for the failure of the present systems of professional development for teachers. Teacher networks are suggested as one possible way to meet the challenge of instructional improvement. Finally, Chapter 7 looks into our near future to consider how technology will improve the student and teacher learning process and our communication with the public. A better approach to curriculum writing and enactment can ensure a better future for our profession, our students, and our society. But when others have confidence in our ability to ensure the return on their investments, it will *bring each of us the personal satisfaction of knowing we did it well!*

There are many people have given me the confidence to proceed with this endeavor. Alice Foster, my editor at Corwin Press, was a constant inspiration. She helped me find the critical kernels and give them zing! Commissioner Richard Mills, Frances Rost, Margaret Goertz, Edward Fuhrman, and Sandra Kolk were gracious enough to review this work in progress and offer helpful suggestions. My wonderfully supportive colleagues at St. Thomas Aquinas College, my students (especially my graduate assistant Doug Doller), and the many teachers and administrators I work with in the Marie Curie Center network keep me close to the realities of teaching in today's schools; they provide rich and responsive feedback on the effectiveness of my communication and accuracy of my ideas.

For reconnecting me intimately to the intricacies of how learning happens, for providing the emotional support that intensive work demands, and for generously giving up some of the time I would have spent with them, I wish to thank my grandsons Joseph and Edward and my husband Mel.

About the Author

Pearl G. Solomon is Associate Professor of teacher education at St. Thomas Aquinas College in Sparkill, New York. She received a doctorate in educational administration from Teachers College, Columbia University. Pearl Solomon has served as a director and officer for professional organizations, and as a consultant to many school districts, the New York State Education Department and the United States Department of Education. She is the recipient of a number of special awards from the state and community for her work in science, math, health and career education

Recent activities include directing the Marie Curie Mathematics and Science Center and its Project McExtend network of teachers in two New York State counties. Eisenhower and Goals 2000 grants that she authored have enabled large scale inservice teacher training efforts as well as Saturday enrichment programs in math and science for 5–12 grade students. Dr. Solomon has presented several papers describing her research in these projects at professional conferences. *The Curriculum Bridge*, Solomon's second book for Corwin Press, is a sequel to *No Small Feat: Taking Time for Change* (1995). The first book analyzed the forces that mitigate the change process and presented templates for implementing productive school change. Her present teaching assignments include graduate courses in curriculum and math and science methods.

1

Weren't There Always Curriculum Standards?

History tells us that the degree of public concern with education has varied through time. As far back as the Egyptians, Greeks, and Romans, and considering as well the carefully prescribed ritual training of youth in tribal societies, formal schooling has been the hallmark of stable human communities. It is a reciprocal relationship, however: Formal education connotes stability, but also bears the responsibility for maintaining it. It is not surprising, then, that in relatively peaceful times, positive public attention is drawn to how we educate our youth and what we teach them. Interest in education grows when there are spare energies and resources to invest. At times of stress, however, attention comes again in response to negative evaluations of the readiness of youth to protect the future. If one generation is threatened, then the next must be prepared to survive. It is the natural order of life on our planet. To guarantee the survival of the species, a plant compromised by drought or disease will often use its diminishing energy to produce the best blooms just before it dies. Either form of attention to education can be constructive, but educational processes have a greater chance of success if they are carefully balanced with viable old and necessary new standards.

With this very brief longer-range perspective of the relationship between education and society in mind, I turn in this chapter to the recent history of this relationship and the rapidly evolving events and setting of the current time. In Chapter 2, "Are New Standards Necessary?" I examine these events and other more stable factors in terms of their influences on school curriculum. An understanding of history and setting is crucial for teachers who must deal with these many and often conflicting influences as they make day-to-day decisions about what and how to teach, and then must deal with the consequences of these decisions. I begin in time at the middle of 1997 and look back at the previous three decades to search for an understanding of the "zeitgeist" of this more recent and volatile episode in the history of American education.

An Educational Forum: Politicians, Kids, and Teachers Offer Thoughts on Education

In his fiscal 1998 budget plan, Democratic President Bill Clinton proposed big spending increases for Department of Education programs. The budget proposal and the State of the Union speech, of which about one fourth was devoted to education, reflect Clinton's emphasis on education and his interest in national standards and assessments. The president's recognition of the need to get the support of states on this issue was demonstrated as he praised the state of Georgia for its academic standards and scholarship program on the day after the speech. He implored that the "American people respond to the challenge . . . to make American education the best in the world, to understand that it won't be done overnight, and not to be afraid of trying to reach higher standards" (Hoff, 1997). What is the American people's attitude toward education? Are they ready to answer President Clinton's challenge? Do they accept his ideas?

Dr. Yash Aggarwal, who was born in Kenya and educated in India, France, and the United States, is a representative of one of the many and ever-changing colors of humanity in my multicultural community. An environmental scientist with a PhD, he nurtured his part-time interests into full-time alternatives. He has been involved and active in community life, working on environmental issues with the town government and the sewer district on a part-time and volunteer basis. This experience and his selection as a spokesperson for the local branch of the American Association of Retired Persons have led to a much more ambitious goal. Yash is now our major party candidate for Congress.

Given his background, candidate Aggarwal's point of view in regard to education is predictable. He believes that we need national standards for education, and cites their existence in other countries, the dissolution of American families, and the failure of American schools as the reasons for this. "If parents don't set the standards, then schools need to do it—school uniforms may not be such a bad idea," he proposed in an interview (personal telephone interview, June 26, 1996). At a recent forum on the topic of education that Aggarwal hosted, some of the participants saw the problem slightly differently. "Part of the problem is the manner in which society sees the education system," said a high school sophomore, and a retired teacher agreed. Another student saw apathy on the part of parents as the root of the problem. "If parents don't care, kids won't." Corey, a high school junior, seemed to agree with Dr. Aggarwal. He didn't believe that teachers were preparing students for the next level, but just making sure they "get by" (Gutwillig, 1996, p. 5).

A parent who was also a teacher lamented that, in contrast to the great changes elsewhere, there was little difference in schools from the way they were 100 years ago. She put the blame for this on the lack of funding to meet the lofty goals of the federal government. Practically everyone at the forum agreed that funding was a major problem for schools (Gutwillig, 1996, p. 5). Money is a limiting factor, but it is not the only one, and it may not be the money itself that makes the difference. To most of us, money represents the public and private interest and values. If education is important, it gets funded. If it is not funded, it cannot be that important.

Funding for education was barely mentioned at a more auspicious meeting held in this same community just 3 months previous to the one described above. The 1996 National Education Summit, which was attended by President Clinton, state governors, and many chief executives of major organizations (but very few educators) focused on the need for and progress toward higher national standards. Public Agenda, a nonprofit research organization, shared an analysis of Americans' attitudes about raising and enforcing higher academic standards in public schools with attendees. The report (Immerwahr & Johnson, 1996) declares that "support for academic standards . . . is at consensus level among the general public," and further concludes that "there is nearly universal support for the idea that public schools do not currently demand enough from students. Americans believe schools should set clear academic standards that significantly raise expectations of students from elementary through high school" (p. 1).

The Public Agenda report, which was based on the authors' own research as well as that of others, contends that this support is shared by all demographic and ideological groups. It further concludes that this support is "unbudgeable" even in the face of "trade-offs" such as the possibility that "some youngsters will be denied diplomas or kept back in school." The authors admit, however, that the endorsement of teachers for the proposals for raising standards is less vigorous. Their prediction is that "classroom teachers are receptive to higher standards, but it is questionable whether they will be the driving force behind them." Immerwahr and Johnson (1996) believe that American teachers are unresponsive to the "deep seated public concerns and values." They believe that these public concerns are in addition to anxieties about the economy and moral decay, and are manifested in complaints about the schools, which have "young-sters graduating without minimum basic skills, truants sporting diplomas alongside youngsters who worked hard" and "jargon-laden announce-ments of yet another educational 'fad.' " They suggest a solution for these concerns: "From the public point of view, raising standards guarantees that students will learn the value of working hard and the penalties of 'goofing off.' And unlike some other proposed educational reforms, raising stan-dards appeals directly to people's common sense" (pp. 1-2).

This report (Immerwahr & Johnson, 1996) is a serious condemnation of the educational enterprise by powerful people who are not professional educators. The focus is mainly on negative results, without regard to the many positive outcomes. After all, how did this country achieve its tech-nological superiority? Moreover, this report limits its analysis of causes for problems to the lack of common criteria for promotion and graduation. It completely overlooks the compounding and defeating effects on the pro-cess of education created by the societal and economic problems it hopes to defeat. It neglects the realities of an issue that is of equal concern to most educators: equal opportunity to learn. It suggests that schools bear the burden for the correction of societal ills even though it offers little respect for the educators who must bear this burden. Somehow, we have missed the boat on the communication of what is good about our schools, and what is needed to improve them. Can negative reports such as these be turned into useful mechanisms for productive change?

Leaders of the business community and governors emerged from the 1996 National Education Summit with an agenda for raising and equaliz-ing standards across the country. This agenda was based on juxtaposed concerns about U.S. economic health and reports of disappointing perfor-mances of U.S. students on international competency tests. Although the test results seem valid, the recommendations for ameliorating the problem are grounded in several powerful but as-yet-unproven assumptions and beliefs about education in the United States, including the belief that the future of this country's economic health depends on the improvement of student achievement, the belief that clearly stated and uniform standards alone will result in higher student achievement in this country when com-pared with student achievement on an international basis, and the belief that high-stakes measures will guarantee the implementation of the stan-dards (McCaslin, 1996; Natriello, 1996).

States have already responded; I discuss further details of this re-sponse in the chapters ahead. Fortunately, states have shown respect for the creativity and commitment of the professional education community by involving it in some of the decision making of the development process. Some teacher organizations have endorsed these efforts, but they are wary about support for externally imposed policies. In a commentary in re-sponse to newly issued standards for New Jersey, the New Jersey Education Association (NJEA), a teachers' organization, compliments the state education department for including the arts, health education, career education, and physical education in the standards, and for "allowing flexibility in how local school districts, educators, and students will work to achieve these rigorous standards within the curriculum" (NJEA, 1996, p. 76). The NJEA cautions, however, that "these standards must be accompanied by an aggressive commitment to providing equal opportunities to enable all students to meet the academic criteria," and asserts that "that can only be done through a responsible state school funding program" (p. 76).

Teacher educators and researchers are similarly optimistic but concerned, especially about the performance measures that accompany the standards. Discussion at a symposium at a recent conference of the American Educational Research Association suggested that we move toward the new standards with caution. Participants related the standards to opportunities for teachers as well as students to learn, and predicted that standards can be useful in proportion to opportunities for teachers to become learners. At the same time, they recommended that visible indicators of school effectiveness be employed, but they should not be used to make negative decisions without evidence of validity. Participants were concerned about the difficulty of producing and administering performance measures that measure what they are supposed to measure. I will come back to the standards and other measures in the chapters ahead, but for now it may be useful to search for the origins of this intense effort to improve schools by raising standards.

The Origins of the Current Wave of Public Concern

Although many writers have identified the National Commission on Excellence in Education (1983) *Nation at Risk* report (often attributed to then-Education Secretary Terrence Bell) as the beginning of this current wave of concern and reform, I suggest that we move back to the mid-1960s and recall that as part of the Great Society changes, Congress enacted the Elementary and Secondary Education Act. This was the first major federal allocation of funds for the purpose of improving education. It encouraged innovation and the acquisition of new resources, and made special provisions for the disadvantaged with its Title 1 (later Chapter 1) part. Surprisingly, this infusion of federal dollars was not in reaction to any great public concern about the failures of schools. It was just the responsible effort of a government in relatively stable economic times to promote the educational process.[1]

In spite of this funding and many successful (and unsuccessful) programs,[2] the 1970s brought us the first evidence of declines in scores on tests, such as the Scholastic Aptitude Test (SAT; now called the Scholastic Assessment Test) and the beginning of public anxiety about education. The SAT and its accompanying achievement tests have been longtime performance standards for the American public. Because they are used by colleges as determining factors in selective admissions, they are examples of high-stakes tests, but private ones, and not derived from state or federal curriculum documents. Many local curriculum policies now reflect their content, however. This was not always true.

In 1976, I participated in a Teachers College (Columbia University) investigation of the possible causes for a decline in scores achieved by the students in two middle-class communities. We conjectured many reasons for this diminution of scores, including esoteric ones such as the birth order of the students in school at the time, and clearly significant ones such as gender. My own hunches had to do with differences in the value placed on the test itself among the students and their teachers, parents, and peers. The results were interesting. Boys considered the test significantly more important than girls, and their results were better. Parent and peer influence had some influence on the scores, but birth order and other contextual factors, such as time spent in last-minute preparation or relaxing the night before, did not have a significant effect. A major finding was that teachers made a difference. In the school district where teachers were newly motivated to place a greater emphasis on the test, there was an improvement in overall scores. There was no attempt to investigate the articulation between the school curriculums and the test; curriculum was assumed to be no different from that for the higher-scoring students of previous decades.

The 1980s brought some new ingredients to the stew over declining SAT scores. Although there was some optimism in the scores for younger students on the National Assessment of Educational Progress (NAEP), the scores for older students were dismal.[3] These were the students who were entering the workforce at a time when competition from other countries became a threat. Several international test reports also showed that the United States was lagging behind other countries in the performance of its students in mathematics and science (see Chapter 2, "Are New Standards Necessary?").

A Nation at Risk (National Commission on Excellence in Education, 1983) also recognizes the possibility of disenfranchisement for those who could not compete within our society:

> Learning is the indispensable investment required for success in the 'information age' we are entering . . . The people of the United States need to know that individuals in our society who do not

possess the levels of literacy and training essential to this new era will be effectively disenfranchised, not simply from the material rewards that accompany competent performance, but also from the chance to participate fully in our national life. (p. 7)

The Response of the Educational Community

The educational community was not unresponsive to these reports. Supported by university researchers, several school districts experimented with effective schools, outcomes-based education, and site-based management. The effective schools movement, which began in the late 1970s,[4] was based on limited research that identified critical factors in schools that had achieved apparent success in spite of adversity in the environments. The research attached school characteristics such as strong leadership; parent, teacher, and student involvement; clearly defined goals and curriculum; a safe and orderly environment; and high expectations to the potential for greater success for *all* students, including those identified as disadvantaged. A number of schools then launched educational improvement plans using these characteristics as criteria for change.

Although the effective schools movement did not have a large-scale following, some criteria were adopted into other school improvement efforts. The idea of clearly articulated goals was at the heart of the outcomes-based education (OBE) reform model. The model gained a fast and strong following, including several statewide efforts—and was probably the source of the notion of national goals. William Spady, who spearheaded many of the OBE efforts, writes that "outcome based education was ushered into the 1990s with a resounding affirmation that this is the paradigm within which true improvement of student learning will occur for all students" (Spady & Marshall, 1990, p. 4).

The pervasiveness of the outcomes-based movement and its attention to a broad base of outcomes, including attitudes and values, may have heralded its demise. Critics, spurred by a small but vocal group of citizens, challenged the outcomes as "too vague, nonacademic, or threatening to family values" (Vinovskis, 1996). The terminology of OBE was quickly abandoned for new terms related to standards and performance measures. By 1993, states that had written the outcome terminology into documents had issued correctives and limited their new standards to the core curriculum areas cited in national goals.

A similar demise may be the fate of another aspect of some of the effective schools improvement programs: the concept of site-based management. The vision that decentralization of power would be helpful in bringing about school improvement also has origins in the 1960s. Large urban school districts such as New York City and Chicago, which had

highly bureaucratized and appointed central boards of education, established locally elected school boards that assumed certain, but not all,
decision-making authority from the central board.

The movement toward further decentralization as a reform in school
governance that would give more power to individual schools and their
parents and teachers emerged in the 1970s in a number of places, including Florida and California. Many of these early programs are still in opera-
tion. Ogawa (1994) identifies a network of actors in the development of the
more recent wave of efforts to engage teachers in site-based decision making, which emerged in the mid-1980s. He labels these individuals working
for organizations as policy actors or *organizational entrepreneurs.* The organizations, which include the Carnegie Forum on Education and the
Economy and the National Governor's Association, were supported in
their efforts by teacher organizations, particularly by Albert Shanker, then
head of the American Federation of Teachers (AFT). Shanker also supported the effort to develop and monitor standards.

Ogawa (1994) credits the rapid spread of the movement to workshops
jointly sponsored by several influential school administrative organizations and the AFT. Although he does not identify universities as in-
strumental in getting the movement going, he does say that it was their
stamp of approval and documentation in articles that maintained the
momentum.

The failure of decentralization to effect educational improvement in
large cities has been mirrored by a similar lack of significant gains from
the empowerment of single schools, teachers, and parents in the more recent wave of governance changes. The large-city efforts have been thwarted
by corruption in both elections and management. The local school efforts
have been hampered by the lack of expertise, resources, and time required
for teachers engaged in the additional burden of managing schools, and by
the unwillingness of those in power to give it to others (Solomon, 1995).

Recent Calls for Reform

Perhaps because of the failure of grassroots efforts to reform education and
continuing reports of declining student achievement, in 1989 the National
Governors Association held a national summit on education and outlined
a major role for the states in educational reform—with a special emphasis
on the creation of standards. A little over a year later, Education Secretary
Lamar Alexander and President George Bush announced the "America
2000: An Education Strategy" national education goals and reform strategy
(U.S. Department of Education, 1991). The introduction to the announcement refers to *The Nation at Risk* (1983) and notes that

we haven't turned things around in education. Almost all our education trend lines are flat. Our country is idling its engines, not knowing enough nor being able to do enough to make America all that it should be . . . we're not coming close to our potential or what is needed. (p. 9)

The original goals state (p. 3) that by 2000,

1. All children in America will start school ready to learn.

2. The high school graduation rate will increase to at least 90%.

3. American students will leave grades 4, 8, and 12 having demonstrated competency in challenging subject matter, including English, mathematics, science, history and geography, and every school in America will ensure that all students learn to use their minds well, so they may be prepared for responsible citizenship, further learning, and productive employment in our modern economy.

4. U.S. students will be the first in the world in science and mathematics achievement.

5. Every adult American will be literate and will possess the knowledge and skills necessary to compete in a global economy and exercise the rights and responsibilities of citizenship.

6. Every school in America will be free of drugs and violence and will offer a disciplined environment conducive to learning.

Two more goals have since been added:

1. The nation's teaching force will have access to programs for the continued improvement of their professional skills and the opportunity to acquire the knowledge and skills needed to instruct and prepare all American students for the next century.

2. Every school will promote partnerships that will increase parental involvement and participation in promoting the social, emotional, and academic growth of children (U.S. Department of Education, 1997).

The goals are accompanied by strategies for their accomplishment. These include "an accountability package based on 'World Class Standards' for each of five core subjects" and a nationwide voluntary examination system in the core subjects. Other strategies include reporting and reward systems such as presidential citations, merit school funding, academies for school leaders and teachers, and differential pay. The document also encourages creative experiments and major commitments by business and local communities.

The goals themselves may be overoptimistic for realization by 2000, and the reality of changing politics has made their realization virtually impossible. Several initiatives were enacted and funded by Congress. Programs for the improvement of math and science education that were previously funded by the Dwight D. Eisenhower Act received new allocations. Grants in specific response to Goals 2000 (in addition to other existing program grants) were awarded for the State and Local Systemic Improvement program, the Goals 2000 program, the Technology Challenge program, and the Schools-to-Work transition program, but each year political wrangling has threatened and undermined well-intentioned plans. Previously allocated money was rescinded, and new allocations are subject to constant revisions. In an unexpected but welcome twist, the 1998 budget compromise provided greater funds for education than any budget since the GI Bill. The effects of this monetary support remain to be evaluated.

In spite of the national goals and the efforts described above, complaints about the quality of education continue. In a report prepared for the 1996 National Education Summit by the National Alliance for Business, author Nelson Smith (1996) quotes the cost to business for continuing and remedial education, and expresses the opinion that it is "an expense that business should not have to bear" (p. 5). Examples of costs given in the report include 10% of $75 million spent by MCI for basic skills remediation; $700,000 spent by Polaroid for basic English and math; and $1,350 per employee spent annually by Motorola. Smith also cites, as evidence of the growing need, an American Management Association report stating that, whereas in 1989 only 4% of American businesses provided remedial training, by 1994 "the figure had jumped to 20%" (p. 5). Smith refers to the hidden costs to business, the overall costs to taxpayers for remedial education, and the ultimate costs to the public for the consequences of poor academic and readiness to work skills: welfare and delinquency. The remedy Smith suggests for all these ills is higher standards and greater vigilance on the part of business leaders.

Responses to the Calls for Reform

Following the Goals 2000 announcement, many state and local efforts were initiated for the purpose of developing and implementing new curriculum and assessment standards. The states have now assumed a major role in this endeavor. In a summary report prepared by the National Governors Association (1996) for the 1996 National Education Summit, 30 states were noted as having completed standards, and 17 states had standards in the process of development. Many others have now completed this work and are in the process of producing matching assessments.

In 1991, the New Standards Project, a coalition of six large cities, 14 states, the National Center on Education and the Economy, and the Learning Research and Development Center based at the University of Pittsburgh, embarked on a major effort to "set very high academic standards for all students, and create a system to measure their progress" (Borthwick & Nolan, 1996). The project was founded by Marc Tucker and Lauren Resnick, with funding from private sources and the states and school districts that form its consortium. Operating under the premise that "what gets tested gets taught," the partners in the New Standards Project believe that better performance measures will increase the possibility of accomplishing high standards, and they have focused their efforts primarily on the production of these measures in the areas of English language arts, mathematics, science, and applied learning.

One of the most successful internal attempts by the educational community to reform education was initiated by the National Council of Teachers of Mathematics (NCTM, 1989). The NCTM produced and disseminated its standards and several supporting materials that have been widely adopted. I discuss the influences of state policies, the NCTM, and other professional organizations in greater detail in Chapter 2, "Are New Standards Necessary?"

A Summary: Systemic Change, Restructuring, and Reform

In an effort to distinguish the recent attempts to change educational processes from previous educational innovations, which may have been superficial and often transitory, the terms *systemic change, restructuring,* and *reform* are most often used—sometimes interchangeably. O'Day and Smith (1993) may have been among the first to apply and define the term *systemic reform* (Vinovskis, 1996). They identified three major characteristics of systemic change:

1. Curriculum frameworks that establish what students should know and be able to do.

2. State policies that provide a coherent structure to support schools in designing effective strategies for teaching the content of the frameworks to all their students.

3. Restructured school governance systems (O'Day & Smith, 1993, cited in Vinovskis, 1996, p. 59).

All the above have characterized the recent efforts to restructure or reform schools. In addition, there has been a focus on the performance measures that monitor the achievement of the standards developed. There is some disagreement about who should develop these standards. Some believe standards should be developed and measured nationally (as they are in other countries). Others believe the states should do the development and measurement, but differ on the degree of flexibility allowed to individual schools in their implementation. Some of the actions neglect to recognize the need for standards for opportunities to learn. There is still a lack of equity in the kind of educational environments that students have available to them, and it seems unfair to hold everyone to the same standard if opportunities and the funds to create them are not equal. These are the issues that were raised in candidate Aggarwal's forum. They are the issues we will have to deal with.

In any case, more than at any other time in this nation's history, attention has been brought to bear on American education. New controls threaten the individual and personal system of classroom instruction that is our legacy from the one-room schoolhouse of the last century. These controls are formidable, and in response to widespread dissatisfaction with accomplishments. The facts on which this dissatisfaction is based may be exaggerated and unfounded—ignorant of the many difficulties faced in a changing social and economic structure. Nevertheless, educators have to respond by knowing and understanding what these facts imply, and by using creative classroom decision-making power to do the most we can to help each child reach for the standards set. This is no easy task, but it is our investment in the future.

Notes

1. Federal aid has come in the form of categorical and block grants. There is evidence that categorical grants aimed at specific purposes are more effective in effecting school improvement (Kirst, 1995).

2. The Rand Corporation (Mann et al., 1975) study of the effects of these programs was one of the first to document the resistance of public schools to attempts to make serious changes (see also Sarason, 1990; Fullan, 1982).

3. The NAEP is a federally managed sampling test. It is designed to evaluate the national program, and does not hold individual schools or students accountable. It is therefore not a high-stakes test. In the 1982 administration, the success rate of students on application questions in mathematics fell 1.1% from an already low percentile of less than 50% in 1978 (Dossey, Mullis, Lindquist, & Chambers, 1988).

4. Ronald Edmonds (1983) and Lawrence Lezotte (e.g., 1981) spearheaded this effort to improve instruction by getting schools to meet identified criteria.

2

Are New Standards Necessary?

Brad should have expected a few of his colleagues to respond this way, but it still came as a surprise. They were nearing the close of a 4-day summer workshop sponsored by the countywide McExtend Network. Many of the participants had been in previous McExtend programs, but this was Brad's first time. More than 100 teachers of all grade levels from 12 different school districts and college faculty had come together to prepare for the writing of curriculum based on the new state standards in math, science, and technology. The general mood was one of decided enthusiasm, tempered by some anxiety about the task ahead. Almost everyone had been inspired by the first part of the experience—especially by the opportunity for hands-on practice with some of the latest educational technology applications.

During the 4-day interval, participants had rotated their venue among several county schools that had new computer labs, and their instructors were the teachers who ordinarily taught kids in the labs. They had worked on new interactive software at an IBM training facility, and seen a demonstration of data bank software by a research scientist. There were sessions in which the new state standards and the new vocabulary were shared. There would be 4 more days of interaction time during the summer and fall for writing and reflecting with each other in small groups.

Brad looked forward to sharing ideas with his grade-level colleagues from other school districts who had joined him at this Goals 2000 federal-grant-funded workshop. Like everyone else, he had heard about the opportunity from his principal, and had volunteered for the task, but he was pleased that the grant would provide some extra compensation for his effort. The first charge was to write a sample curriculum unit based on the new standards that participants could use and would try in their own classrooms. These units would then be shared electronically among the whole group via a Web page. Later, back at Brad's own school, two other colleagues, Meg and April, would join Brad in the task of creating a whole curriculum for the grade.

The openly expressed complaints from teachers that surprised Brad reminded me of the difficulty of effecting change in schools with top-down policies. A negative comment about the time outside of the 4 days required for typing the new curriculum at first seems to be an example of a nonprofessional attitude, and quite different from the anxious and honest comment from a high school teacher that there was no room in his course of study for another unit. I realized, however, that both protestors apparently saw the new state standards and testing mandates not as a way to improve what they were doing, but as externally imposed, perhaps unnecessary add-ons, and apart from their normal agendas and responsibilities. There was little "ownership," and teachers were consequently resistant.

This reaction may be an illustration of what Richard Elmore (1983, 1987) calls "the power of the bottom over the top," but I believe that the manifestation of this power of active or passive resistance to change is a result of the failure of policymakers to understand the many and often conflicting influences on teacher autonomy and the curriculum decisions that they make. This chapter examines some of these influences in an attempt to know them better and consequently to understand why some people believe that standards are necessary and others do not.

Some Charismatic Differences of Opinion

Teachers rarely see their rather private world in the classroom as a microcosm of surrounding society. Nor do they clearly recognize the power of its influences. They are more likely to be concerned about the need to reach and control their students, the next administrator's observation, or uncooperative parents. Although teachers and administrators may not have taken state-developed curriculum guidelines seriously in the past, new monitoring and enforcement measures attached to the new standards may cause them to put these in proper context with the many other already existing traditional influences. Knowledge is power, and perhaps a greater understanding of the way in which external influences affect day-to-day curriculum decisions would be useful to teachers such as Brad, Meg, and April.

For example, it would be useful for them to know that their individual struggle for autonomy within their own setting is part of a larger conflict in which public schools are currently engaged: the debate over control of local school curriculum. In some respects, this debate mirrors our country's continuing conflict between two of its democratic ideals: the Jeffersonian ideal of political equality, in which the majority controls and protects the public rights, and the realism of Alexander Hamilton, who recommended an economy of free competition in which individual private rights take precedence and the powers of centralized government are strong. The conundrum in this tension is that free competition distributes wealth unequally and places too much power in the hands of the few—and this then undermines the public rights (Labaree, 1997). Has big business influenced the new effort to reform education?

In politics, conservatives usually take the Hamiltonian position, and liberals take the Jeffersonian ideals. In comparison to these positions, school conservatives seem to prefer the controls of national standards, and cautious liberals are more likely to hold the line for local and teacher autonomy (Unks, 1995). In a Public Agenda interview with national leaders (Lehmann & Spring, 1996), Donald Stewart, president of the College Board, said standards are necessary because we need to answer the question "Are we better in terms of something?" (p. 3). Former Assistant Secretary of Education and conservative school policy spokesperson Chester Finn added that "standards are only meaningful if you also answer the question 'How good is good enough?'" (p. 6).

There are pockets of resistance to government-imposed standards among some conservative groups, however, as well as support for them among unlikely liberals. Albert Shanker, the late head of the American Federation of Teachers (AFT), was in favor of mandatory state standards. He rationalized his opinion in the Public Agenda interview (Lehmann & Spring, 1996):

> I think that third grade students should all be expected to learn certain things because that's part of what lends authority to standards . . . When you create elasticity, you also create a questioning attitude as to whether what you're doing is important or not. (p. 17)

In support, authentic testing advocate Grant Wiggins (1995) defines standards in terms of their implication of "a passion for excellence and quality," and he describes a school with standards as having "high and consistent expectations of all learners in all courses" (p. 187).

The ideological struggle increases in its depth and diversity as society becomes more variegated and complex, and perhaps diverts attention from the real needs of schools and students. The teacher in the one-room schoolhouse had only slightly more autonomy than most teachers have today, but the pressures to infringe on that autonomy and efforts to protect it are now much more intense. The general public is concerned about the apparent failure of U.S. schools to compete favorably with Asian and European nations on international measures. Businesses, facing a shortage of technologically proficient personnel and challenged by the need to provide training for growing numbers of employees in what they deemed to be basic skills, rally to support the feelings of mistrust of the public education enterprise. Politicians pick up on the issue. Governors and the president make the improvement of education a major part of their agendas. Delaine Eastin, the California state superintendent of public instruction, takes her responsibility with a global perspective:

> The reality is that we not only need to be able to compare across our nation—which we get in a hit-or-miss way through things like the SAT or ACT scores—but we need to be able to compare across the globe, so that we know that California's children can compete with the German and the French and the Japanese children. (Lehmann & Spring, 1996, p. 3)

The Media Influences Opinion on Standards

A vigilant media recognizes the sensitivity of the American public to any threat to its economic and military dominance, and increases the intensity of its coverage. It casts aspersions on conscientious teachers such as Brad, Meg, and April, who begin to feel less confident and more resentful and resistant. It makes boards of education, concerned about their constituents' support, more vulnerable to the temptation to make hasty and ungrounded decisions. What is wrong with what they are doing? Why do outsiders see national standards as a solution to the problems?

Mortimer Zuckerman (1996), the editor in chief of *U.S. News and World Report*, asks if we are content as a nation to be second, third, or fourth, and if we place greater importance on the self-esteem and happiness of our children than on what they know and can do. He accepts the financial constraints of a growing population and costs, but admits that we need to get better results at the same time. Zuckerman makes a valid point about the mobility of our population, and identifies higher and uniform national standards as the needed solution. "Science does not change because it is taught in Oregon or Florida" (p. 128). He decries the "dirty little secret" (p. 128) that we already have informal national standards in that we all use similar lessons and textbooks, and then argues that these represent minimal competency rather than the higher levels expected by other countries. Zuckerman also presents the underlying agenda that many educators suspect in his prediction that "higher standards are the key to inducing performance-based innovation and performance-based assessment of teachers and administrators" (p. 128).

The press substantiates its position with the views of noted scholars and grassroots proponents. Diane Ravitch of the Brookings Institution notes that "nations that establish national standards do so to ensure equality of education as well as higher achievement because they make explicit what they expect children to learn to insure that all children have access to the same educational opportunities" (cited in Mosle, 1996b, p. 47). Another article (Mosle, 1996a) tells the story of Michael Johnson, an urban principal whose school curriculum is based on preparation for the standardized tests he sees as gatekeepers for his students. He is glad that his teachers forced him to take subjects that seemed irrelevant, and believes that his kids want direction. Mosle (1996a) cites author Lisa Delpit, who in writing about African American students says that they "need skills, not fluency . . . I'm sick of this liberal nonsense" (p. 42).

It is this notion of greater equity that has popularized the idea of standards among minority populations and aligned minorities with conservatives. But leaders among these populations are suspicious of the more subjective performance assessment measures that in some cases have been attached to new standards (see Chapter 6, "How Are We Doing? Measuring Success"). They believe that standardized tests are fairer, and that minority children need the "hard skills" they measure.

The Liberal Reservations About Standards

Some teacher groups and teacher educators bristle in response. Keith Geiger, president of the National Education Association, agrees that teachers should be held to high standards, but only if they receive the proper funding support for their professional development and if they have the primary role in writing standards (Lehmann & Spring, 1996).

Others question the basis for the push toward standards. Berliner and Biddle (1995) believe that there is no real crisis in education, and see the imposition of standards as a threat to local educators' autonomy. They wonder why we criticize ourselves in the press, and contend that the crisis is a "manufactured one" and a "big lie." Bracey (1996, 1997) challenges the authenticity and interpretations of international test results. He points out that there is greater variation within nations than there are differences between them, and that although the United States is a little behind in mathematics, it is ahead in reading. When the test results are confirmed and his objections are partially answered by researchers, he asks whether Americans want their children pressured like Japanese children to achieve the same results.

Presenting the philosophical view of the debate, Kenneth Strike (1997) identifies one picture of national standards as an expression of a kind of nationalist communitarianism, a "view that believes that we need more of a shared culture" (No. 11). But he warns that this picture of standards may put limits on the scope of the curriculum with his caution that "alternatively, we might claim that national standards assert only content that is objectively true or widely held and that is, therefore, neutral to our diverse cultures and moral and religious traditions" (No. 11). Strike also reflects on the work of Chubb and Moe (1990), who contend that schools work better when teachers are organized as teams and the climate is participatory, and that teachers need higher levels of local autonomy.

In an earlier publication, Strike (1993) espouses a Habermasian view of democracy in which decision making is face-to-face and discursive. He fears that, because the standards movement takes discussions about what is educationally worthwhile into national or state forums, the educative community is left only with the charge to implement distally decided programs—that may or may not be relevant to immediate needs. Strike (1997) conjectures that "in an educational system in which there is a stronger sense of community and ownership, efficiency will be easier to achieve." He further conjectures that "perhaps we need to focus more on what makes schools good communities and less on what makes them efficient organizations." His final objection to the standards movement is that it views students as consumers of a service and as resources for national productivity wars who need to be motivated to comply with system expectations. The standards movement does "nothing . . . to transform student interests or to reduce their level of alienation and disengagement."

In spite of the reservations of the liberal view, efforts to identify and monitor educational standards are well on their way; the ball is rolling, and with a momentum that may be difficult to stop. Will standards achieve greater equity? Are they effective in other countries? That depends on what kinds of skills we want equity for and what we deem effective. Will national standards make a difference? That depends on the opposing influences, on their authority or enforcement methods, and on the ability of educators such as Brad to translate them into local curriculum policy, accept ownership, and make the standards work.

Standards in Other Countries

In other countries, where the private rights democratic ideals are not as ingrained, the imposition of national constraints and rules is less likely to be counteracted by active and passive resistance. As an example, consider a law passed in 1996 by the German government that officially changed the way certain words are spelled to ease the difficulties that children had in using correct spelling. The law did not just make a recommendation; it provided for sanctions of teachers and officials who disobey. Although there was some debate on the issue (some felt it did not go far enough), there are firm deadlines for implementation. Newspapers, publishers, and others are gearing up for the change. Contrast this with our nation's century-long debate over a switch to the metric system. We are now the only developed country not using it.

Borthwick and Nolan (1996) identify six qualities of national standards in countries that outperform us. Their standards are specific, public, rigorous, high stakes, inclusive, and measurable. Japan identifies precisely what core knowledge content is to be covered—but leaves much of the detailed instructional decisions to teachers. In the Public Agenda Interview (Lehmann & Spring, 1996), Diane Ravitch of the Brookings Institution talked about the Japanese national standards as a model of simplicity: "They are so much simpler and clearer and more challenging and more direct than anything I have seen from American standard writers." Albert Shanker, of the AFT, agreed that "standards have to be doable." California's superintendent of public instruction, Delaine Eastin, reported that plain language is a criterion for her state's standards: "They will be very useful, usable and readable—they won't be written in Edu-speak" (p. 11).

Japan's standards may not be verbose, but the power of its government-prescribed spiral curriculum is further driven by the Japanese University Entrance Examinations, given in three stages. There are also differences in the instructional components of curriculum. Japanese teachers emphasize problem solving in math, whereas American teachers and their textbooks have been more concerned with facts and procedures. The Japanese teachers are also more likely to engage students in reflective discussion, to include fewer but more real-world questions that require extended answers, and to provide students with manipulatives (Stevenson & Stigler, 1992).

Japanese textbooks also do a better job of what Mayer, Sims, and Tajika (1995) call "cognitive modeling" than American textbooks. They show students how to work out problems in detail instead of devoting space to unexplained exercises involving symbol manipulation. Most Japanese children spend much more time on homework than children in other countries, and also go to private after-school coaching programs called *jukus* that prepare them for the exams.

France's curriculum is published and widely available. Its yearly exams are followed by much public discussion of the questions and the results. Although Sweden has tests, they are not as rigorous as the high-stakes *baccalaureate* of France and the *arbitur* of Germany, both of which determine student access to further education. In contrast to the beliefs of many Americans, other nations not only have caught up with us in terms of secondary student retention, but have insisted on uniform expectations with rigorous tests, even for those not planning higher education.

In 1988, Great Britain embarked on a major endeavor to develop specific syllabi in every subject area (due for completion in 1997). In 1993, it instituted an elaborate school inspection system with a follow-up support component to help deal with diagnosed problems. In the United States, the operations of a number of failing city school districts have been taken over by state governments.

Surprisingly, with the exception of The Netherlands, where there is elaborate tracking of students and a free choice school voucher system, the standards for students in Japan and the European nations are the same for all students (Unks, 1995). Even in Germany, where at a relatively early age students are tracked into three different schools with varying emphases on the pure, the practical, or the applied, the curriculum is the same. Still, as Unks (1995) notes, the curriculum in the countries studied resembles that of the United States in that it is subject centered, and "the evidence is weak, suspicious, or nonexistent that the study of any particular school subject (as it is usually conceived and taught) promotes outcomes such as critical thinking, creativity, citizenship or many other desirable goals" (p. 425).

We in this country already have a variety of public and private standard-setting, inspection, and testing systems in place, but they are inconsistent. Growing public discussion suggests that consistency, or at least the inspiration for it, should be generated at the federal level, but formal mandates are another matter. If history is our teacher, then we can predict that in this country these will come at a different level.

Influences on Curriculum:
State Legislatures and Education Departments

Following the 1994 and 1996 National Summits on Education, many states leaped onto the standards bandwagon. At the time of the 1996 summit, only three states did not have new standards and matching assessments in place or in progress. These actions are in line with tradition and with the constitutional allocation of control of education to the states. In contrast to many other countries, the U.S. constitution gives states the right to manage education, and they have taken up the cause for standards with vigor.[1] If the federal government has had any influence on what has happened in individual states, it has been by virtue of its allocation of funds. For example, much of the funding for improvements in math and science education and for the development of new state standards has come from federal funds appropriated as part of the Goals 2000: Educate America Act. But a provision in this act that calls for the creation of a federal panel that would approve model standards that states could consult in writing their own versions was opposed by the Republican party. Because of those objections, President Bill Clinton never appointed the members of that panel and eventually agreed to abolish it.

Probably the boldest and most controversial proposal in Clinton's 1997 10-point plan (whitehouse.gov/wh/html/library/html) to improve education was to encourage the creation of voluntary new tests based on the reading test of the National Assessment of Educational Progress (NAEP), which has been given in the past on a controlled sample and volunteer basis to assess the progress of our nation's schools, and the math portion of the Third International Math and Science Study (TIMSS), an international and worldwide comparison that includes 25 industrialized and developing countries. Clinton suggests that these would allow states to gauge whether students are meeting national standards of excellence in those subjects. One hopes that this emphasis on testing national standards will not incite the struggle to define the role of the federal and state governments in education.

The February 12, 1997, edition of *Education Week*[2] (Hoff, 1997) reports the mixed reactions of Republicans and Democrats. Governor Roy Romer of Colorado, general chairman of the Democratic National Committee, says that Clinton's program will not create the federal intrusion that many critics fear: "He's saying: 'In order to make this work, you need to have a test.' " Romer further notes that the proposal "preserves for the states . . . the kind of education policy that people want to keep at the local level." In his speech, Mr. Clinton advocates "not federal government standards, but national standards." Some Republicans also supported the president; Governor John Engler of Michigan, a prominent Republican spokesperson on education issues, endorsed it.

Within a short time, state leaders in Maryland, Michigan, West Virginia, Kentucky, and North Carolina promised to offer the assessments once the tests become available in the spring of 1999, and other cities and states soon joined them.[3] Some states were not ready to do so. "Nebraskans fancy themselves as very independent," says Kathleen McCallister, the president of the state board of education, "Nebraska is not real trusting of Big Brother." She expresses her faith in local decision-making with this comment, however, "If a local school district wants to offer Mr. Clinton's tests, you're not going to see this board stand in the way. The bottom line is: That's a local decision." A comment from Republican Representative Robert L. Livingston of Louisiana strangely echoes the position of liberal education leaders: "The federal school board is not what we need to be . . . we need to give the resources to the teachers in the classroom." Another representative concurs: "What we don't want to have are national standards that are mandated and national tests that are mandated" (Hoff, 1997).

Considering the fact that many states and professional organizations have already embarked on ambitious assessment plans for their own standards, a push for federal mandates does not seem to be a battle worth fighting. Most states are skirting the issue of mandated standards, and instead are preparing extensive assessments, which in effect create mandates. Nebraska and some other states in the Midwest and West take particular pride in their independence, and state officials do not have the constitutional authority or political inclination to issue a testing mandate. New York has a long history of regents examinations required for endorsement on respected, but optional, regents diplomas. Commissioner Richard Mills is a staunch advocate of higher state standards. He is leading the effort to add new forms of mandated regents exams and eliminate the minimum competency alternatives. The state also has a concurrent plan for changing high school graduation requirements. The greatest value in the whole standards movement may be that we all look more carefully at our expectations for our students.

In its introduction to its new standards, the state of Wisconsin provides a position statement with a rationale and clearly set direction for implementation and enforcement (Wisconsin Department of Public Instruction, 1996). The statement is representative of the many state documents that have been produced or are in process, and appears in Table 2.1. All the state documents imply the need for accountability and appropriate measures. Several openly recognize that some of their substance was derived from the work of professional organizations such as the National Council of Teachers of Mathematics (NCTM) and university-based groups such as the New Standards Project. Many also recognize the need to involve teachers and parents at the local level. But where do the local school boards stand in this apparent show of state authority over education?

Local Control of Education

In an analysis of evidence for a shift of control of curriculum from local school districts and teachers to state governments, Tyree (1993) describes the ways in which state governments manifest their authority. He identifies these ways as law, expertise, norms, tradition, or the charisma of politicians. For example, Florida and Texas have passed legislation that stamps their curriculum documents as law. But Florida's curriculum documents are not very specific, and therefore leave much to local districts and teachers to decide. Florida has little in the way of sanctions to enforce the law, and does not imply the credibility of experts in the production of its

TABLE 2.1 Position Statement of the Wisconsin State Standards

- The public cares deeply about education.
- For parents, business, and taxpayers, the bottom line is what graduates know and can do.
- The public wants, and their elected representatives demand, educational accountability. Accountability requires clear statements about what students are to learn.
- If educators don't write clear, explicit and rigorous standards, someone else will.
- To have credibility, educators must provide evidence of effective academic performance by public school students.
- There will be statewide assessments. If educators are to have a meaningful role in these assessments, they must communicate with the public and elected officials.
- Effective education requires standards—clear statements of what is to be learned.
- The general citizenry should determine those targets of education with advice from educators.
- Educators are best equipped to determine how those targets are to be met.
- Judgments about the effectiveness of education should be based on student knowledge and performance.
- The primary purposes of assessment are to improve learning and to provide accountability.
- What is assessed is what gets taught (and learned).
- Assessment should cover the full range of learning described by academic standards.
- Effective assessment systems measure complex thinking and applications as well as basic knowledge and skills.
- Assessments must be credible and technically defensible.
- Public disclosure of assessment results should focus attention on learning that will lead to its improvement.
- Schools and districts should be evaluated on results rather than on inputs. The need for various inputs can be determined only when assessments have established a base line against which attempts to improve learning can be tested.

SOURCE: Wisconsin Department of Public Instruction (1996).

documents. Nor does Florida have a tradition of state control like that of New York, with its explicit and extensive curriculum guides, regents exams, and graduation requirements.

Texas, on the other hand, has laws and sanctions. It also has some normative authority in the long-term consistency of some of its curriculum. California has no law, tradition, or norms to give it authority. It does have much expertise and a pioneering spirit to try new things. This may create problems. Authority without law has been invoked in New York, New Jersey, Ohio, Illinois, and Maryland, where states took over the management of deficient city school districts. These cases may demonstrate that in the long run, money has power. The withdrawal of state funds for local administration allows this to happen.

At the national level, President Clinton may be the best example of an attempt to use charisma to gain authority. Within a month of his call for volunteers for national assessments, states and city school districts representing 20% of the nation's school population agreed to give them a try. Tyree's (1993) conclusion, however, is that although there is a potential for states to channel or reduce local curriculum options, much decision-making power still remains at the local level.

The next question is, where at the local level? Anne Bryant, the executive director of the National School Boards Association, and Paul Houston, the executive director of the American Association of School Administrators, discussed their definitions of the relative roles of school administrators and the political entities that engage them (Bryant & Houston, 1997). Bryant sees the school board role as "establishing a vision" and "taking the conversation to the community." In reference to state standards, she feels that schools should be asking how they can "go beyond the standards." Houston says that the relationship between the board and its administrators should not be adversarial, and that it is the administrator's function to deal with the public.

In a document published in 1990, before the current emphasis on standards, the New York State School Boards Association (NYSSBA) expressed a similar role for boards to set the tone and direction for the district's curriculum by developing a curricular philosophy, policy, and goals. They recommended that the board should hire and evaluate administrative personnel "based on their ability to provide leadership for curriculum planning, development, implementation and staff development" (p. iii). The NYSSBA document also suggested that state curriculum guides should be consulted, but that the state should allow more flexibility to local districts. The tone of this may have changed within the past 7 years, but careful examination of recently completed New York standards documents and messages from the commissioner reveal that there is still much to be decided at the local level in terms of specifics.

Nonetheless, teachers have to pay attention to the sanctions of high-stakes tests for their students and yearly state report cards that expose students' performances and their own performances to public view. This brings to the educators, the teachers, and the administrators the task of creating the specifics of the curriculum in the context of prescribed visions, leveled and measured expectations, and the many other nongovernmental influences.

Influences on Curriculum: Professional Organizations and Universities

The charge of writing new state standards-based curriculum was a new one for Brad and his colleagues. They were more accustomed to writing individual lesson plans—often derived from the text they were using, a favorite grade-level theme, or some professionally developed curriculum package. Like Sara Mosle (1996b), the New York City teacher who wrote a pro standards cover article in the *New York Times Magazine*, they recognized that original curriculum writing required time, energy, and devotion. Although recognizing that teachers did not necessarily implement the city's prescribed experience and theme-based curriculum the way it was intended, Mosle discounts its value and yearns for the textbooks of her childhood. This is typical of distally produced curriculum documents. In practice, they are rarely used as intended. Teachers tend to adapt them in fragments for their personal use. The state documents that Brad, Meg, and April had been handed when they first were hired or when new ones were published had uninteresting and unclear formats and did not seem to relate to what their students needed, and they were given few supporting materials or implementation ideas. These materials certainly did not compare to the textbooks, with their extra activity workbooks and teachers' guides.

There had been a districtwide emphasis on the standards of the National Council of Teachers of Mathematics (NCTM, 1989), but these seemed to be a more general thrust that encouraged a greater focus on mathematical reasoning, problem solving, and using manipulatives. The teachers in Brad's district did not view the NCTM standards as a curriculum (it was not intended to be one), or even as the basis for writing one of their own. The district had arranged for several staff development workshops in which staff were given suggestions for use of a variety of math manipulatives. The new texts had many more problems and pictures, and the questions were more challenging. Teachers still needed to get the students prepared for the computations on the standardized tests, however, and therefore supplemented the texts with worksheets.

For many years, professional organizations such as the NCTM have had a palpable and growing influence on curriculum. Much of that influence has been indirect, principally through publications and conferences.

Many teachers and schools subscribe to the organization's periodicals, which contain brightly illustrated and well-presented ideas for lessons and units at all levels. Teachers try the suggestions of their colleague writers, and sometimes they contribute suggestions and articles of their own. Teachers also look forward to and enjoy conference experiences. It makes them feel like professionals, and gives them the opportunity to communicate on an adult level with new people in different settings. They often come back refreshed and enthusiastic to try the new ideas to which they have been exposed.

The NCTM standards document was an exception both in its premise and in its wide acceptance by the educational community. There are several reasons for its success. To begin with, there was immediate support from the business community, which was concerned about reports of the failure of U.S. students to compete on an international basis with students in other countries, as well as its own frustration with mathematically unprepared employees. The Second International Mathematics and Science Study (SIMSS) report (see McNight et al., 1987; Schmidt et al., 1996) revealed that performance on international tests by U.S. students was about average when compared with other countries involved in the test. It is well below countries such as Japan, Korea, Hungary, and Canada. The report also revealed that mathematics curriculum in this country was less focused and emphasizes arithmetic rather than more challenging topics such as algebra and geometry, and that our schools devoted less time to mathematics had lower expectations, and in contrast to 85% of the other countries evaluated, no uniform standards.[4] The National Assessments of Educational Progress showed similarly disappointing performances, especially among the older students (Dossey et al., 1988).

The timing of the NCTM document was most propitious in its issue immediately following these reports, but there are other reasons for the success of its standards:

- They were developed by a teachers' organization, and therefore received the immediate support of teachers and school administrators. It was a set of recommendations by teachers for teachers.

- They state in a very clear and forceful manner what is right for math education.

- Mathematics is a value or issue-free content area that is subject to little local variation or cultural difference.

- NCTM, in contrast to other organizations, has a broad spectrum of membership that includes college mathematicians and teacher educators, as well as primary and high school teachers.

- The statement was not a prescribed curriculum monitored by mandated measures.

Although many school districts initiated professional development programs in response to the NCTM standards, colleges used them as a basis for the preparation of preservice teachers, and even textbook publishers responded, the evidence is minimal that there has been a long-term effect on student achievement or teaching practice. Part of that lag may be due to a lag in the local assessment forms (see Chapter 6, "How Are We Doing? Measuring Success"), but it may also be due to missing elements of professional development (see Chapter 7, "Where Do We Go From Here?").

In contrast to the success of the mathematics standards, similar national efforts in science and social studies have thus far had less success with wide dissemination and adoption. *Science for All Americans: Project 2061* (AAAS, 1989) was published by the American Association for the Advancement of Science (AAAS), which is an association of professional scientists and university professors. It had support from private organizations such as the Carnegie Foundation and several states for the purpose of developing standards in science. The original Project 2061 document was supplemented by *Benchmarks for Science Literacy* (AAAS, 1994). This is a comprehensive content-focused curriculum intended to "identify a minimal core of critical understandings and skills" that constitute science literacy.

These standards never gained widespread recognition or acceptance. The missing involvement of K through 12 teachers may have slowed acceptance. Science teachers organizations, which do not have much representation from higher education, did not take ownership of the benchmarks. Science teachers tend to be fragmented into the different science areas and, therefore, present a less cohesive force for change.

Another prestigious organization of scientists, the National Academy of Sciences' National Research Council (NRC), issued its standards document in 1996 (NRC, 1996). With an emphasis on scientific inquiry and a call to teach science the way science itself is done, these standards were closer to the agenda of science educators. There was also attention to assessments and a better organization than that of the AAAS documents.

Perhaps the coldest reception and reactive furor followed the publication of the *Curriculum Standards for Social Studies: Expectations of Excellence* by the National Council for Social Studies (NCSS; 1994). These were certainly not value or issue free. New York Education Commissioner Richard Mills explained his preference for traditional subject area organization:

> You can easily get lost in this, and it has caused some people to get very touchy-feely-fuzzy about what they expect. And that has opened the standards movement to charges from more conservative folks who worry about government and school intruding into issues of values. (Lehmann & Spring, 1996, p. 8)

In its attempt to be politically correct, the NCSS document precipitated the first vehement protest against standards. In spite of the furor created by some of the inclusions and lack of them, several states used much of the NCSS work in developing their own documents, but carefully explained that new inclusions did not exclude other important items.

Most of the publications of standards by professional organizations have been used as the basis for the state standards documents. In a survey of the status of arts education, Peeno (1995) discovered that 49 states used the standards issued by the National Art Education Association (1994) as a guide and resource for their own curriculum documents. They have also learned lessons from them. The introduction to the Colorado history standards explains why it includes world history:

> The Colorado Model Content Standards for History address both world and United States history, including the history of the Americas, and may very well necessitate reorganization of the social studies. The inclusion of content from world history and the history of the Americas suggests that all students should participate in instruction in these areas. The inclusion of areas of the world that have often been neglected in the study of history is in no way intended to exclude the continued study of western civilization and its significant place in the history of the United States. Because of the increasing interactions among all nations of the world and the effects of these interactions on our daily lives, it is imperative that students have knowledge of the history of both our nation and that of other nations. (www/stst/colorado.html)

Several professional organizations and state standards documents also recognize that standards are not enough, that schools must also do some reeducation and reorganization. A world languages study group considering the inclusion of special education students in language classes realized that this will require extensive training for language teachers. The Massachusetts state standards clearly recognize the need for reorganization:

> Both the Common Core of Learning and the Curriculum Frameworks state that change in the classroom is directly related to how schools are organized for learning. The Common Core of Learning and Chapter Two of this framework advocate an instructional focus based on inquiry, problem solving, and learner-centered classrooms, all of which have implications for how schools schedule instructional time. The expectation that each and every student should achieve high standards has implications for how schools group students. Similarly, teachers cannot integrate the strands of

social studies unless there are longer classroom periods to accommodate extended discussions, Socratic dialogue, and primary source research. (www.stst/massachussetts.html)

Influences on Curriculum: The University

Leadership for the standards movement has also come from a traditional source of influence on the curriculum: professors in teachers colleges and universities. Aside from their major role as teacher educators, universities have had an important influence on the substance of what is taught in schools as well as on instructional methods. Unfortunately, even though it usually has good intentions, that influence has been inconsistent, uncoordinated, at times obscure or incoherent, and always tenuous, subject to the charisma of its guru and vacillating interest in the latest fad. Many good educational researchers separate themselves from practitioners, and practitioners are often intimidated by the special language and quantitative parameters of research. A few individual faculty members, who have a better understanding of the nature of the classroom, successfully pitch their ideas with good marketing techniques. A profession hungry for ways to deal with the ever-more-challenging task of educating a diverse population buys their ideas.

Neither the teachers nor the professor innovators are to be blamed or held blameless. Sometimes what seems like an intellectually sound idea is not effective in the hands of an unskilled or resistant practitioner. Follow-through and follow-up classroom support to help teachers struggling with a new technique or curriculum are rarely provided. The inadequately implemented new ideas are quickly pitched for the next interesting innovation (for further thoughts on innovation and change, see Fullan, 1990; Sarason, 1983, 1990, 1993; Solomon, 1995). Some notable exceptions include the long-standing effect of science curriculums produced by the Biological Sciences Curriculum Study, which originated at the University of Colorado, and the Science Curriculum Improvement Study, which originated at the University of California at Berkeley. Several universities are currently producing and piloting math programs that meet the NCTM standards.

There has been widespread support from professors for local school programs that employ the whole language approach to reading and writing, but a recent backlash of pressure from a few conservative educators to restore phonics as the major emphasis in learning how to read caused the rollback of California's 10-year-old whole language program. A recent heated discussion on the controversy among university authorities at a conference of the International Reading Association can only undermine teachers' confidence and fuel undercurrents of mistrust for the approach among parents, who have had different learning experiences. Among the whole language detractors at the conference was a publisher of phonics books, and among the questioning parents were some who had been subjected to radio commercials for Hooked On Phonics. Phonics never were eliminated from the whole language concept, but their place in the program was not clearly delineated or understood by some teachers and many parents. This lack of comprehensive knowledge and communication makes everyone subject to the competing lure of the marketplace.

A mechanism for exerting influence on curriculum used by teacher education institutions is their role as facilitators and instructors for inservice education. Although much of this has been haphazard and subject to the varying demands of a competitive marketplace, networks of teachers and schools that include higher education institutions offer a better solution. The summer workshop that Brad attended was planned and organized by the McExtend network of local schools and a local college. The college took a leadership role in consolidating the separate efforts across districts and got some needed outside funding to form the network. The agendas of the college and the schools were synchronized, and teachers had the opportunity to learn in a new, comfortable, and nonthreatening environment (see Chapter 7).

On a much larger scale that involves a large university, whole states, and urban cities, major groundwork for the standards movement has come from the New Standards Project, described in Chapter 1, "Weren't There Always Curriculum Standards?" The New Standards Project has focused not only on the standards themselves, but on the development of coordinated assessments that combine conventional and alternative forms (see Chapter 6, "How Are We Doing? Measuring Success"). Through the project, standards and terms have become models for much of the work at state and local levels.

Influences on Curriculum: Commercial Materials

Commercially published curriculum materials include books and their supplements, kits of hands-on materials, and software for computer assisted instruction. They may appear in more holistic organized form or in small fragments that teachers incorporate in many different ways. These materials dominate teaching practice in this country (Ball & Cohen, 1996). They are the "stuff" of lessons and units. When teachers choose or are assigned texts, they often accept the text as their curriculum. The text then constrains and controls knowledge and teaching.

The quality of modern texts is questionable. In a scathing criticism, Tyson-Bernstein (1988) calls them superficial, with unexplained facts and missing contexts:

The prose is dumbed down to accommodate the poorer reading skill; faddist and special interest group messages, however meritorious appear as bulges or snippets of content; flashy graphics and white space further compress . . . text. (p. 194)

I have on my bookshelf an early 1940s science text, written by the renowned science educator Morris Meister. It has little white space and black-and-white pictures. But it has superb and interesting narrative and well-developed ideas. Its form and content are worth considering for a new and better generation of texts.

The power of texts as an influence on curriculum is evident in states that have textbook adoption policies, which limit teachers' choices. These large states then have an influence on what is published and what is available in other places. Publishers are not totally to blame; they publish what sells. If educators made different choices, the market would respond.

Teachers cling to these commercial materials because they help them maintain control and relieve them of the burden of creating original materials all the time—but they still take great pride in the original materials they do create, and resist attempts to deprive them of that freedom. Reformers sometimes use commercial materials in their attempts to change what teachers do. In actual practice, confronted with great variation in their students and personal skills and their imperative to maintain autonomy, teachers tend to adapt rather than adopt the reformer's materials.

Technological items, including satellite interactive video, graphing calculators, and computer software, will probably be the major form of instructional material in the near future. Preparatory hardware in the form of classroom computers has been a major investment for the nation's K through 12 schools in the late 1990s. These schools spent an unprecedented $4.34 billion on computers in 1996, an amount that is expected to double by 2000 (IDC/Link).

Some of the new educational software is a decided improvement over the previous generation's drill and practice on screen. I recently viewed programs that use real science databases, observed students take original measures in a wind tunnel in a smart technology lab, and watched 2nd graders do PowerPoint presentations and 5th graders embellish them with video clips. I have put students in touch with research scientists over the Internet, and had them read the e-mailed poetry of a class in Africa. Educational software and Internet sources may replace much of the traditional materials of the classroom of the near future, but for a while at least, they may face the same problems as previous materials: lack of quality, insufficient teacher skill in their use, and overdependent and uncreative engagement with them by teachers and students. To be effective, they have to be connected to the achievement of standards that are desired, to what we know about how learning happens, and to the real lives of the students they teach serve. I will further discuss the tremendous potential, but yet unproven promise, of technology in the chapters ahead.

Ball and Cohen (1996) identify five intersecting domains that define the influence of materials on teachers as they enact their curriculum. They omit two important influence domains: knowledge of how learning happens and assessment; I address these in Chapters 3, "What We Now Know About How Learning Happens," and 6, "How Are We Doing? Measuring Success." The domains Ball and Cohen identify include the political context in which teachers function, as discussed above, teachers' knowledge of individual students, and the social environment of the group, which will be addressed in following chapters. Two domains of influence on materials that they also include are related to teachers' autonomy: Their own understanding of the materials and the way they fashion them for students. Individual teacher autonomy has been a major influence on school curriculum.

Influences on Curriculum: The Teachers' Right to Choose

My friend Diane teaches in a special education program in an urban area. She often complains of the unbending bureaucracy with which she has to deal to get things done. One day she mentioned that her program card had to be posted on her door. "What is a program card?" I asked. She quickly replied, "Well, you know, it says that you are going to be teaching 30 minutes of reading and 30 minutes of math and that you will have two periods of art for the week and so on—but it's all nonsense for these kids. I just try to keep them busy and motivated." Diane is a conscientious and effective teacher. Her honest belief is that control structures such as the program card are just for show, something to justify the administrative role. She has no compunctions about doing the right things, the things she believes her kids like and need. In spite of the structures that may put limits on the environment in which she acts, she has autonomy over the real stuff of learning because there are no real measures of her compliance and her effectiveness, nor sanctions for not being effective.

Diane's experience is not an aberration—although there are exceptions, and a strong push toward standards and accompanying measures may change this. It was confirmed as illustrative of the existing status in a recent study by Glass (1997) and in studies by Darling-Hammond (1990) and Sedlak, Wheeler, Pullin, and Cusick (1986). Darling-Hammond notes previous studies that reveal that "regulations were imprecisely and differentially followed from place to place" (p. 234). In reviewing an analysis of implementation of mathematics changes in California, she notes that teachers viewed the new curriculum framework as a policy statement handed to them by administrators with new locally approved textbooks. "As a consequence . . . teachers were unsure of what the policy really consisted of, and what it meant for their teaching . . . they had too little information . . . and too little opportunity to discuss their ideas with others" (p. 236).

Most of the teachers in the large McExtend group with Brad had not seen the new standards for which they were supposed to write curriculum. Others had seen them, but had difficulty understanding their organization, and had no clear ideas about how they were supposed to respond to them. Their plans before this workshop were to do what they had done in previous years—their own thing.

Comparing the status of teachers' control of curriculum with previous times, Glass (1997) cites from Sedlak et al. (1986), who found that teachers today enjoy more freedom and autonomy than their predecessors. The professional codes of conduct of the 19th and early 20th century, which were much more controlling and enforced by administrators, are no longer the standard. As a beginning teacher in 1949, I was told to wear a hat and gloves to school and to turn my weekly plan book in on Monday morning. My principal had it in front of her when she came to observe.

In retrospect, however, I remember that I didn't always follow my plan or feel that compelled to do it when my principal wasn't sitting there. The experiences reported by teachers in the Sedlak et al. (1986) study support the popular belief that once they close their classroom doors, teachers are "able to exercise enormous discretion" (p. 121). Despite what might be construed as constraints imposed by the larger bureaucracy of state departments of education on public schools or large district-level administrations, public school teachers frequently maintain autonomy. Like Diane, they take control and experience freedom in a bureaucracy by ignoring, working around supposed constraints, or using "passive circumvention" (p. 120). They use their ingenuity and skill to circumvent mandates.

Even if new state standards and district curriculum documents attempt to set limits to the range of possibilities available to teachers, it is doubtful that they will remain within them. In the Glass (1997) study, one teacher responded to a question in reference to state-mandated curriculum standards:

You have the standard things you go by . . . but for the most part, it is pretty much that you do your own thing. . . . You shouldn't impose (curriculum) upon teachers, but let teachers be more creative. On the district level we have curriculum that we must follow . . . but the core curriculum is only meant to be about 60% of the curriculum. Forty percent of the curriculum we can decide on. (No. 1)

Glass (1997) also questioned teachers in reference to their relationship to school administrators.

> One time school administrators imposed an in-service program on us. We behaved so badly they have, since then, let us determine what goes into them. So I would say currently we have a great deal of control. I resist bitterly and strongly changing my teaching style . . . I resist and I do it either overtly by speaking out—expressing it; or, if that fails, one can very simply do it covertly in the classroom. Simply not do it. Chairs still exist, but we are more of a local autonomy school now. We have a committee that meets and decides things with the principal. The state has a list that they give out to districts. The department discusses the different kinds of textbook . . . but individual teachers make their own choices. (No.1)

This seems to minimize the power of school administrators, and contradicts the findings of the literature that effective schools have strong principals. Strength does not always come from using power, however; it can come when power is given through support and opportunities for responsible decision making and capacity building. Many of the participants at the curriculum workshop that Brad attended had been encouraged to attend by their principals, and indicated in follow-up assessments that principals' support was critical in being able to implement the new curriculum. In the Glass (1997) study, principals concurred with the impressions of the teachers:

> Everything that I do is a collection of information and input from teachers in this building, the department chairpeople in this building . . . They give me an awful lot of input. I'm constantly asking them for direction. While the public school expects teachers to follow the district curriculum guides, they are just that—guides. An established curriculum does not mean there is no room for innovation. The presence of a curriculum does not deny creativity. (No.1)

In his study, Glass (1997) does not indicate whether or not the autonomy the teachers have is a result of formal involvement in site-based management. In a previous book (Solomon, 1995), I reported on the benefits and difficulties of personal experience with a structured engagement of teachers in the decision-making process. There were decided benefits of diminution of teacher isolation and a growing sense of professionalism for teachers so engaged. And as Chubb and Moe (1990) discovered, teachers in my experience made some excellent and productive curriculum decisions for their students. Among the problems that I identified were the lack of willingness of those in power to share it, the reluctance of teachers to accept responsibility for their decisions, and the failure of schools to provide teachers with the necessary resources such as new skills in consensus building and time needed for their engagement in the management process. There have been mixed reports of success with ventures into formal structures of site-based management. Perhaps teachers and their organizations have not pushed so hard for this is because they already have autonomy—without all the work.

Influences on Curriculum: Parents

Parents have an uneven effect on curriculum and teacher autonomy depending on the socioeconomic structure of the community. For example, parents wishing that their children gain admission to prestigious colleges may exert influence on schools to offer advanced placement (AP) courses and produce National Merit Scholars. Surprisingly, these parents may also be apprehensive of innovations that stray from the traditional core curriculum, especially if they are nontested subjects or concepts. They want their children's schools to be copies of the ones that brought them success. In an attempt to implement a new standards-based math program, I experienced resistance from parents whose children already were doing well with rote computation. They distrusted manipulatives and wanted more worksheets to come home (Solomon, 1995).

Parents who are consumed with the expectation for high achievement are more likely to serve on district committees and to pressure administrators to make changes. Many of these changes will be related to their individual child, however, rather than to the school program as a whole. These parents will pressure principals to place their children with teachers whose classes achieve high scores or in honors classes. In school districts with upper socioeconomic populations, some teachers feel more intimidated by parents than by their administrators. The parents are their day-to-day monitors. The teachers in these situations consequently make curriculum decisions that will appeal to parents. A teacher in the Glass (1997) study described how pressure from parents to prepare students for an AP exam undermined her right to select her own curriculum and in effect diminished the value of her professionalism, expertise, and training.

Getting Ready to Design Curriculum

As Brad, Meg, and April embarked on their task of writing curriculum that meets the new state standards, they brought a history and habits of practice framed by the many influences described above. To help understand those influences, they might wish to seek answers to the following questions.

- What exactly are the federal, state, and district mandates that exist?
- How are they enforced?
- What tests are based on them?
- What do the experts say about the curriculum I need to address?
- Do I agree with them?
- How will parents view this curriculum?
- Do I know how to use the materials I need and will they be suitable and available?
- What kind of support will I get from my administrators?
- How much autonomy do I have to decide on the specifics of this curriculum?

In response to this chapter's title question "Are new standards necessary?" I trust professionals such as Brad, April, and Meg and readers to come up with their own answers. But with all those influences pulling in different directions, some consistency in knowing where one has to go might be the light at the end of a dim tunnel with many branches. I know that the place where I want to go has to do with learning, and before I make any decisions about curriculum, I want to know how learning takes place. I come to this next.

Notes

1. The State of California, which got a head start on establishing the NCTM standards and on changes to whole language approaches has had to deal with some repercussions to these and this slowed implementation of statewide standards in all subjects. Other places such as Alberta, Canada, have openly dealt with protests to their new mandates.

2. *Education Week* may be accessed on-line at www.edweek.org.

3. At this writing, eight states and at least five large cities have agreed to use national standards-based tests. This represents about 20% of the nation's school population.

4. The Third International Mathematics and Science Survey (TIMSS) reveals some improvements, especially in science, but still finds the United States trailing other countries in student achievement and much less focused in its curriculum (see Schmidt et al., 1996).

3

What We Now Know About How Learning Happens

Serendipity is not to be taken lightly. Just as I am putting the finishing touches on this chapter, state legislation has been introduced to require recertification of teachers every 3 years, and the reason given for this legislation is that teachers need to be updated on educational theory. In Chapter 2, "Are New Standards Necessary?" I addressed the many influences on teachers' curriculum decisions. Although some of these influences often begin as distal or indirect, they are quickly transferred to the more direct effects of local power, school organization, and leadership. But what about the science of teaching, the theory and the practices, that researchers have proven as effective—do they influence us? Are those as easily transferred?

This chapter shares a sample of the emerging ideas of educational philosophy and the findings of cognitive research that could have a powerful and proximal influence on instructional decisions. But history has shown us that this influence often has a limited and transitory effect, unfortunately. Although researchers are constantly engaged in exploring how learning takes place and evaluating the effectiveness of various educational strategies and contexts, their findings are only rarely transferred broadly to educational practice. The roadblocks that make the transfer of a few new ideas easy and many others difficult are elusive and unpredictable. They may be a factor of the nature of the competition within the research community, and perhaps its relative isolation from and lack of respect for practitioners. My own rationale for the disparity in how research findings are translated into practice has less to do with the quality of the findings and more to do with the charisma of the researcher-salesperson.

Human resistance to change in institutions we cherish and trust in their original form also makes the transfer of such new knowledge difficult. The great variations and fluctuations in the culture, politics, and philosophy of schools and their need to respond to individual differences in human beings and their social interactions add further complications. These situational variables are not ignored in the research; along with the other variables of the learning process, they are treated in a less than holistic fashion, and not always clearly connected to each other. This is, perhaps, an example of the modernist focus on the specialization of knowledge (Doll, 1993). Such specialization accounts not only for the lack of connections within the research base itself, but, more important, for a consequent loss of value to the teacher, who must deal simultaneously with all the variables.

An example of the difficulty in making holistic connections is witnessed in the fall 1993 edition of the *Review of Educational Research*. An attempt by Wang, Haertel, and Walberg (1993) to organize the disparate elements of educational research into a comprehensive knowledge base is followed by several articles that either refute the suggested organization or declare the endeavor impossible to achieve. Similar (perhaps semantic) philosophical dialogues about the existence of knowledge and reality and whether or not the acquisition of new knowledge is situated (confined to a particular context and not readily transferred to new situations) appear in recent editions of *Educational Researcher* (Anderson, Reder, & Simon, 1996, 1997; Greeno, 1997).

Such discourse may be stimulating to the research community and in the long run produce a more tested theory, but it has not helped those who are immediately accountable for practice, and it has weakened the prospect of incorporating the findings of research. Teachers are already resistant to change and wary of new ideas derived from research as panaceas for their problems because many of these have proven unrealistic in their real school applications. They don't know who to believe!

Nevertheless, many of the findings are valid and should be considered valuable contributions to our understanding of how learning happens; and because I believe that it *is* possible to transfer this generalized knowledge to the new situations each teacher confronts, some of these ideas are presented here. This is not meant to be an inclusive survey; there is much that is omitted. Instead, I have selected some of the more holistic and seminal findings that can be woven into a simple framework that can help guide teachers in making curriculum decisions.

To help focus directly on connections to practice, I extract a series of *knowledge construction curriculum applications* from these findings in this chapter, and in the following two chapters refer back to them as I address the mechanisms of constructing curriculum.

I begin with some of the current epistemology or thinking about the nature of knowledge. A review of recent cognitive science theory on the general nature of intelligence and brain function and some more specific findings on motivation, control, and interest follows. The role of human goals as controllers of the process of constructing new knowledge is then identified as a significant and unifying connection between the cognitive science and the philosophy. Finally, there is a summary of the theory and its connections to the curriculum.

An Exciting Conference

Meg and April talked animatedly with colleagues from other schools at the conference luncheon. Dr. Gardner's ideas on multiple intelligence seemed to make so much sense.[1] They had fun doing the morning activities that allowed them to explore their own intelligences. Meg commented, "I always knew I was better at the spatial things. It was easy for me to come up with the picture . . . but forget about mathematical logic." April responded, "Remember the conference we attended on right and left brain research? I wonder which intelligence is where? Does this mean that my kids who are good at art can't think logically? How about Leonardo da Vinci?" Meg retorted, "I do not think Dr. Gardner meant to say that at all, but it would be so hard to change our lessons to meet every kid's needs. And think about the standardized tests; they are so verbal or mathematical. Can you imagine giving kids an alternative of drawing a picture?"

Meg and April walked away from that conference alerted to something that may have made an impression, but probably resulted in little long-term change in what they were doing in their classrooms. Although progress has been made because based on theories of multiple intelligence, some teachers are adding variety to their activities and forms of assessment, the recent emphasis on standards and their measurement poses a threat to innovative and difficult-to-measure departures from tradition—*unless the standards call for them.* There is much to warrant such a call. The nature and scope of knowledge and its accessibility have changed dynamically; so must our educational enterprise.

Educational Philosophy: Piaget and Constructivism

Although they are usually treated separately, educational philosophy and cognitive development theory often overlap, and better integration could be most useful. The branch of philosophy that explores the nature of knowledge and knowing is *epistemology*. The notion that knowledge is self-constructed had early origins in the ideas of Locke (see Longstreet & Shane, 1993; Orton, 1995), but is most frequently connected to the work of Jean Piaget (1926, 1977). Piaget considered himself a child psychologist (Piaget, 1926, p. xx), and much of his early work is based on clinical observations. His later work tries to integrate what he learned into a more generalized explication of knowing, and therefore many would classify him as an epistemological philosopher.

Piaget's (1926, 1977) work is frequently misinterpreted. He is most readily identified with sequential stages of cognitive and moral development, and these stages have often been (justifiably) refuted as more flexible or mutable than some of us originally believed. Less emphasis has been placed on Piaget's later ideas on the construction of knowledge; recently these, too, have been misinterpreted. Piaget believed that knowledge is self-constructed. *Real comprehension of a concept . . . implies its reinvention by the child. . . . It is important first that the child should have been able to find, by himself, the reasons for the truth that he is expected to understand* (Piaget, quoted in Ginsburg, 1989, p. 96). Such statements have been interpreted to mean that knowledge construction is a highly individualized process, not a social one.

Piaget (1926, 1977) may not have meant this at all. Although he believed that these reinventions, or "schemes," are at first based on actions with objects, he carefully observed children in their discourse with others in the environment, and attributed the construction of schemes to their interactions. He concluded that at early ages, most new schemes are internalized, but not really shared in conversations with peers. Early language is monologic or a collective monologue. The child, with a companion at her side, is essentially talking to herself, but uses the language expression to help internalize the scheme. As time makes the child less egocentric, language becomes adaptive—it is listened to and responded to—and then the child and the construction of new knowledge become more responsive to social interactions (1926). Piaget never discounted the role of the teacher or parent. Reinvention "does not mean that the teacher (or parent) is useless, but that his role should consist less of giving lessons than in organizing situations provoking investigation" (Piaget, quoted in Ginsburg, 1989, p. 97).

Following is a guiding knowledge construction principle that we can extract from the research and thoughts of Piaget.

```
KNOWLEDGE CONSTRUCTION CURRICULUM APPLICATION 1

The curriculum should provide experience-rich environments
that promote opportunities for students to learn with under-
standing as active participants, rather than environments that
rely on passive students and teacher telling. Dialogue among
peers should be encouraged even if it is at first monologic.
Technology and manipulatives should be employed to provide
the richest possible active environment.
```

Recent Interpretations of Constructivism: Radical Constructivism

Recent interpretations of constructivism build on both individual and social elements. A more individualistic and radical interpretation is that
each of us constructs his or her own schemata: bits of knowledge, explanations, or pictures of reality according to their fit with our individual
goals, previously existing concepts, and new perceptions (von Glasersfeld,
1990). This definition also builds on the work of Ausubel (1963, 1968),
who recognizes that before new knowledge can be absorbed or reinvented,
it has to fit with what is already there and be chosen by the learner.[2.]
Learning, from that perspective, is much more under the control of the
learner and less likely to occur when information is fed in an unconnected
way into a passive learner. The learner must take ownership.

```
KNOWLEDGE CONSTRUCTION CURRICULUM APPLICATION 2

The curriculum should pay attention to and address students'
prior knowledge and their goals. New perceptions are needed
to create new knowledge. A teacher cannot just feed informa-
tion and expect it to be absorbed because the learner has to "fit
it in" to what is already there.
```

Radical constructivists argue further that there is no one real truth or reality. They contend that knowledge is different in each of us because it has been situated in a highly individualistic learning experience, subject to the variations of prior knowledge, genetics, and perception. From this perspective, Meg and April would walk away with completely different concepts of Gardner's talk and their own conversation.

This radical constructivist interpretation has created a conundrum for some cognitive researchers and practitioners, who depend on empirical measures of learning as the basis for their findings and practice. How does one measure learning that is different in every individual? If reality is so individualized, what is the role of the adult, parent, or teacher as a communicator of culture? Does this perspective deny the validity of well-grounded research that demonstrates the effects of social intervention on student achievement?

Social Constructivism

The ideas of Vygotsky (1978), the Russian psychologist, present a more socially interactive picture of the construction of knowledge. He places a stronger emphasis on the sociocultural context and the role of mediators. In his theory of cognitive development, Vygotsky distinguishes two types of learning experiences: those that occur from the bottom up, giving rise to "spontaneous concepts" that are undirected and unimpinged on by adults, and those that result from adult-generated or top-down activities that produce "scientific concepts." He suggests that these two types of learning inform each other, and that learning takes place when the child's knowledge and adult structures approach each other in a "zone of proximal development." The adult or other mediator sets a learning environment of objects and spoken dialogue that stretches the child above his or her present knowledge level toward a higher level. Eventually, the stretching becomes internalized and the child reaches higher-order thinking levels.

Other researchers (e.g., Wertsch, 1979) have expanded on Vygotsky's (1978) ideas with demonstrations of an interactive process that connects the bottom-up experiences of the child and the top-down dialogue of the adult in what they term a *scaffolding* process. Resnick (1983, 1989) uses the term *instructional mapping* to describe how teachers might use dialogue and manipulatives to help students make the connections between their informal experiences and formal schooling. In a recent application of this to the teacher's role in setting the stage (or planning) for the construction of new knowledge by children learning mathematics, Steffe and D'Ambrosio (1995) suggest that teachers create a *zone of potential construction*. This is a kind of prediction of the *zone of proximal development* that is based on the teacher's knowledge of what the child already knows and experience with how other children learned. Planning for such a zone would require teachers to make better use of their assessments.

The cooperative learning environment, which has been proven effective by many researchers, incorporates the social contexts needed for learning implied by Vygotsky (1978), and it supports or supplants the direct role of adult mediators with peer mediators. In the cooperative learning setting, peers can construct mutual zones of proximal development in a context of interactive discourse where social goals of affiliation (being part of the group) and personal goals of efficacy (feeling that one can do something) enhance the chances of new knowledge construction (Johnson & Johnson, 1989; Johnson, Johnson, & Holubec, 1987; Sharan et al., 1984; Slavin, 1987, 1990).

KNOWLEDGE CONSTRUCTION CURRICULUM APPLICATION 3

Learning environments should provide a multitude of social interactions such as those provided in cooperative learning or artifacts such as interactive computer programs. Teachers need to plan to stretch their students' knowledge across the zone of proximal development or construction, carefully matching environments, prior knowledge, and planned outcomes or standards.

A Compromise

Some constructivists have attempted a compromise between the radical and social constructivist philosophies with the recognition that social processes mitigate the individual construction of knowledge (Figure 3.1). This was suggested by Piaget (1926, 1977). The child learns when his or her thoughts are listened to and he or she receives a response. Cooperative groups may be doing more than transferring what each knows to the other, however; they may be learning new things together. Schemes that are newly constructed for each interactor in a shared process have been defined as intersubjective. Lerman (1996) argues firmly for intersubjectivity in the acquisition of knowledge. He quotes Vygotsky's (1978) argument that "the true direction of the development of thinking is not from the individual to the socialized, but from the social to the individual" (p. 136).

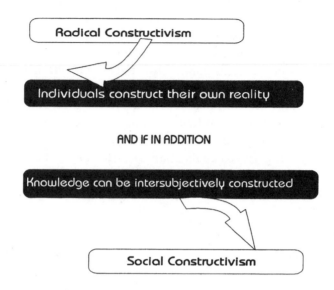

Figure 3.1. A Philosophical View of Knowing

Lerman, in his own words, continues, "When an action gains significance for a child, becoming bound up with goals, aims, and needs and associated with a purpose it is a social event" (p. 136).

Meg and April then would collectively construct new knowledge based on their experience and their conversation, knowledge that might not have been constructed had they not had a social interaction, and this knowledge would be new to both of them and to Dr. Gardner, whose reality in regard to intelligence may also be quite different from other cognitive scientists. Cobb (1990) ascribes the realities that we hold in common and use to communicate with each other to the "consensual domain." When Meg and April discuss the seven intelligences suggested by Gardner in school the next day, they know what each other means when the term *logical/mathematical knowledge* is used; it is in their consensual domain. The standards we choose as we collectively construct curriculum for our students come from our consensual domain.

Even when they are formed in social interaction, however, individual pictures of reality may or may not be correct as judged by comparison with what most other human beings see as reality. The instructional process then becomes a matter of bringing the learner's reality closer to the reality of the teacher—a social process of helping the individual develop, confirm, or correct his or her own schemata or reality pictures so that they approach the realities of the consensual domain. I address the applications of the social construction of knowledge more specifically in following chapters, but a guiding principle follows.

KNOWLEDGE CONSTRUCTION CURRICULUM APPLICATION 4

In addition to the knowledge transferred from individual to individual so that it may be shared and in a consensual domain, knowledge new to each may be constructed in interactions. Curriculum content standards should consist of the knowledge of the consensual domain that educators judge as appropriate for the individual and learning situation; the enabling standards and activities of the instructional process should be considered a way of building and correcting individual realities.

Constructivism provides an overall way to look at knowledge and knowing; it tells us that prior knowledge, new perceptions, and human goals are factors in creating new and individual knowledge. It does not tell us how to construct the specifics of our curriculum or deal with the differences in our students, but it sets the stage for further study and understanding. And it raises further questions. For example, if new knowledge is constantly being constructed, how does the construct of in-place intelligence fit into the paradigm?

The Changing Nature of the Concept of Intelligence

Back at school, Meg and April continue their discussion about Dr. Gardner's talk. Meg wants to know how to measure the seven different forms of spatial, logical/mathematical, bodily kinesthetic, linguistic, musical, interpersonal, and intrapersonal knowledge, and asks, "Do you then average them? How will I know what to expect of my students? How will I know if I have made some progress with them?" April responds, "I always thought that intelligence was something you were born with and couldn't change; but didn't he say something about nurturing the different forms?"

Early debate among cognitive scientists was similar to the above discussion. It contemplated the origin of intelligence in the individual and its nature. Debate centered on whether intelligence is innate and inherited or

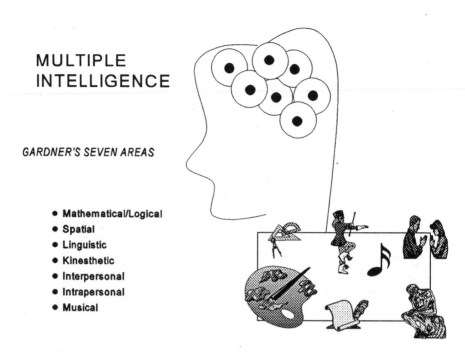

Figure 3.2. Multiple Intelligence: Gardner's Seven Areas

acquired in an acculturation process; whether it should be accepted as a psychological entity or merely a mathematical abstraction that can be used to measure individual differences (Lohman, 1989). The present consensus concerning intelligence is a compromise that accepts the presence of some innate psychological or physiological components, but also recognizes the powerful influences of the environment. Current debate focuses more on the various typologies, such as Gardner's (1983, 1993, 1995), that propose multiple subsets of the construct of intelligence and on the hierarchy of skill levels and their developmental sequence.

Multiple Intelligence Theories

This dialogue, as yet unresolved, has led to several theories or models of intelligence. They are all modular, seeing the brain as having multiple intelligence forms and/or levels. They also introduce such variable factors as what is considered as intelligent behavior in the particular culture and the influence of previous experience with similar situations. In contrast to the wide recognition and effects of Gardner's (1983, 1993, 1995) ideas of multiple intelligence (see Figure 3.2), other ideas are less recognized by practitioners. They are, however, highly respected by researchers and have helped change some of our notions about intelligence.

INTELLIGENCE IS A COMPLEX DYNAMIC CONSTRUCT

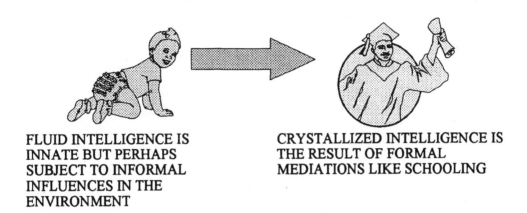

FLUID INTELLIGENCE IS INNATE BUT PERHAPS SUBJECT TO INFORMAL INFLUENCES IN THE ENVIRONMENT

CRYSTALLIZED INTELLIGENCE IS THE RESULT OF FORMAL MEDIATIONS LIKE SCHOOLING

Figure 3.3. Dichotomy of Fluid and Crystallized Intelligence

In an early compromise between the concept of intelligence as an innate construct and its acceptance as an acquired one, Cattell (1963) hypothesized intelligence to comprise a "fluid" ability that is "physiologically determined" or innate and a "crystallized" ability that is the result of the fluid ability interacting with experiences in the environment. Crystallized ability then is measurable intelligence. Cattell's dichotomy of fluid and crystallized intelligence (Figure 3.3) is widely accepted and incorporated into other theories. It essentially moves from the notion of a passive and immutable or in situ image of intelligence to a more active process of cognitive development that fits well with constructivist ideas.

Some interesting new research that President Clinton picked up on as rationale for funding early intervention programs discovered that the extent and nature of human interactions in the first year of life have a profound affect on future ability to learn (Bruer, 1997; Nash, 1997; www.ed.gov/pressreleases/ Oct 31, 1997). This seems to confirm the Cattell (1963) theory—with one exception. There is evidence that there are physiological reasons for this. Apparently, brain cell growth is incomplete in the newborn and stimulated by human interaction in the first year of life. Is this then fluid or crystallized ability?

Horn (1985) also questions the innateness of fluid ability. He believes that differences in fluid ability reflect differences in casual learning or independent thinking (perhaps the spontaneous knowledge described by Vygotsky, 1978), whereas crystallized ability differences reflect differ-

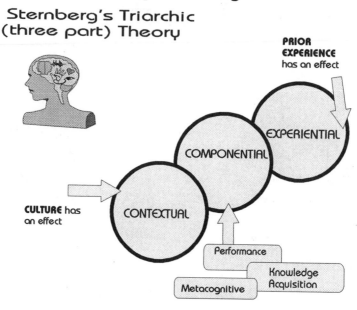

Multiple Intelligence

Sternberg's Triarchic
(three part) Theory

Figure 3.4. Sternberg's Triarchic or Three-Part Theory

ences in acculturation learning—the differences in the child's experience
(Vygotsky's scientific knowledge). Promoting the idea that intelligence is
a multiple or modular construct, Horn describes other factors of intelligence such as perception, retrieval, speed, and processing, but places fluid
and crystallized ability at the top.

Sternberg (1985, 1988) defines intelligence as the mind's ability to
govern itself, and presents a triarchic modular theory that has three sub-
theories (see Figure 3.4). His contextual subtheory connects the assessment of skills as intelligence indicators to their recognition in the culture
as desirable and practical (Sternberg, Okagawa, & Jackson, 1990). An implication of this concept relates to intelligence tests. They are based on
western culture and emphasize linguistic and logical-mathematical skills.
Other cultures may value the interpersonal (social) or intrapersonal
(knowledge of self) skills identified by Gardner (1983, 1993, 1995) more
highly. Middle-class suburban parents may view skill in mathematics as
an important indication of intelligence. The parents of urban ghetto children may see their children's interpersonal street survival skills as evidence of their intelligence. Recognition of the role of cultural values as
criteria for judging intelligence has had growing acceptance, and to some
this makes present testing systems invalid.

Sternberg (1985, 1988) also describes a componential subtheory. He sees intelligence as composed of varying levels or components of cognitive function, and identifies these as metacomponents, performance, and knowledge acquisition components. The metacomponents control the other two, which produce actions and acquire information. Performance components carry out the plans and strategies of the metacomponents. They use inference, application, and comparisons to respond to information and relate it to concepts in prior knowledge. The performance components also work interactively with knowledge-acquisition components, which perform a sorting process to evaluate and categorize new information. Together, these lower-order components send information back to the metacomponents.

In his third, experiential, subtheory, Sternberg (1985) gives weight to experience with a situation. Repeated experience moves a situation from novelty to automatization, and coping with novelty is an integral part of intelligence. Whereas novel situations require attention, automatized responses allow diversions to other concurrent inputs or tasks. Meg, who is an experienced teacher, has automatized her patterns of classroom dialogue. She can concentrate on the responses her students are making and analyze the problems metacognitively. April, less experienced, must struggle with what she is going to say next. She gropes for a quick solution to problems (Rosko, 1996).

Neither Sternberg's (1985) nor Gardner's (1983, 1993, 1995) model focuses on innate individual differences as distinguished from acculturated or acquired differences. Nevertheless, although it may be politically discomfiting, genetic research provides growing evidence of some predetermined personality and physiological tendencies that may affect crystallized intelligence.

In addition, neither theory suggests a hierarchical sequence of skill development levels that preclude parallel development of lower-order skills and relatively complex or higher-order thinking. This supports previous questions about some of the interpretations of Piaget's early work. Research in mathematics education has also demonstrated that it is not necessary to learn algorithmic procedures to solve complex problems, and that it may be better to learn or reinvent the procedures (if necessary) after confronting and understanding the problems (Fuson et al., 1997; Heid, 1988). Concrete experiences may be needed at various ages for some new constructions, but even toddlers can reason abstractly. I remember my grandson at age 2, when cautioned about the danger of the swimming pool in my backyard, saying, "Is that like the hot stove?" He made an abstract connection between two very different situations and generalized the concept of danger. Taken as a whole, modular intelligence theories have several important implications for curriculum.

> KNOWLEDGE CONSTRUCTION CURRICULUM APPLICATION 5
>
> Intelligence is a complex characteristic influenced by some inherited traits, but also profoundly subject to the influence of environmental experience. It is not one limited set of abilities, but a variety of them. These abilities may exist and vary in different areas such as linguistic and kinesthetic, or in different phases of processing such as metacognitive controls or sorting and organizing information. The sequence in which these abilities develops in different areas or phases is not hard and fast. Individuals may vary in their power among the contents and the processing phases. Curriculum should reflect this variation among individuals in its support of already-existing ability and in the further development of all abilities.

The Information Processors

Intelligence is something we usually think about in the passive sense, but its value is in its ability to act, and it can be measured only by virtue of its actions. It makes sense, therefore, that intelligence theory should have the same patterns that learning theories have. Sternberg's (1985) componential subtheory reflects the work of those who study information processing: cognitive psychologists who study the brain's processing functions and use computer analogues to explain how learning happens. A great deal of this research is connected to the computer scientist's desire to achieve artificial intelligence (AI)—or the ability to simulate the human brain with advanced computer technology. In support of these efforts, there is also basic research on how the brain functions physiologically.

Like Sternberg (1985), the cognitive scientists propose several different mechanistic levels of brain function that correspond generally to the architecture of the computer. There are different parameters and nomenclatures for the levels, but scientists agree on their presence. A better understanding by Meg and April of how these levels function may be as helpful as knowing that there are different kinds of intelligence, and may be critical to the potential improvement of the whole schooling process. Unfortunately, even though some of the levels such as the metacognitive controls of learning have been studied in several research contexts, the findings have thus far had little influence on classroom environments.

Surprisingly, the information processing ideas may even present a resolution for the philosophical debate between radical and social constructivism: whether reality exists only as an individual construction or as the shared reality of the consensual domain. The outcome of the debate may, as Orton (1995) suggests, be of little consequence to educational practice because the new knowledge offers a compromise between constructivist philosophies. It provides a supportive empirical base for each philosophy. The work of John Anderson is but one example of this base.

In support of Piagetian ideas, Anderson's (1983, 1990) adaptive character of thought theory unifies previous research on modular brain processes by positing that processes are all part of the same system: individual subsystems, or levels, code information from the senses to form representations or frames in the memory. Anderson notes the adaptability of memory to revise or recode these representations in response to new situations, and calls the revised representations "adaptations." These may correspond to Piaget's (1977) notion of accommodations as new constructions of knowledge. Current physiological research on brain function suggests that these adaptations or accommodations probably occur as a result of synchronous timing of brain actions in which previous memory frames are retrieved at the same moment in time as new messages from the senses (Blakesley, 1995).

Like von Glasersfeld (1990) and the radical constructivists, Anderson (1990) believes that several levels of cognitive processes are governed by human goals. At the top level of brain function, he places a rather iconoclastic (in cognitive science) rational level—distinctly human, and therefore not analogous to present computers—that recognizes goals and causes cognition or learning to operate "at all times to optimize the adaptation of the behavior of the organism" (p. 28). In other words, the human brain adapts its behavior so that it can best accomplish its goals in each given environmental situation. Anderson describes human goals as controls of the selective retrieval of previously stored adaptations, and suggests that it may be unnecessary to know how the brain does its lower workhorse functions if one can predict on the basis of its rationality how it will respond in a given environment.

Explanations of how different environments influence what the human brain sees as optimal need to be explored, but we have some ideas from previous research and practical experience. If Meg knows that her students will more likely be motivated to retrieve prior knowledge by a problem that concerns *Nintendo* games than by a problem that concerns books on a shelf, she will write Nintendo problems. It is also not much of a stretch to realize that the social environment can create and modify the goals that constitute Anderson's (1990) rational level. Most children will have goals that lead them to prefer social interactions and goals that make

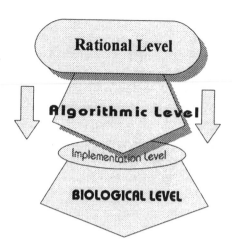

Figure 3.5. Anderson's Architecture of Cognition

them compete or comply with their social group. Knowledge of what a student sees as optimal may be of the greatest significance for teachers as they create the learning environment of their classrooms.

Anderson (1990) hypothesizes that the bottom or biological level of brain function is analogous to the computer's machine language, and corresponds to the neural function of the brain. It is the workhorse of production—carrying out the instructions provided by two or three upper levels: the implementation level, the algorithmic level, and the rational level. The algorithmic level contains the brain's programming directions. This is where prior knowledge is accessed from long-term memory and new perceptions are categorized and connected, perhaps to previously formed or newly constructed generalizations (such as the 2-year-olds). This is where adaptations happen. The implementation level is placed tenuously between the biological and algorithmic levels as a sort of holding place. Anderson hypothesizes that it may not even exist (see Figure 3.5).

Because of difficulties in identifying the nature of the biological and implementation levels' corresponding processes in the human brain, Anderson (1990) does not think these levels are ultimately important in the explanation of human cognition. Empirical physiological evidence of the nature of regions of the brain certainly does not make a comprehensive theory based on understanding the biological level easy to come by. If, as reported by scientists studying minor stroke victims, the verb form for the word *march* is stored in a different place than the noun form for the word, and one may lose one form without losing the other, then it is unlikely that knowledge must be developed in a sequentially fixed pattern. The brain also seems to be adaptable, with damaged areas being replaced in completely different places.[3]

Anderson (1990) has great hopes, however, for the algorithmic level,[4] which outlines steps that must be taken and helps form the goals of the rational level. I begin discussion of the role of human goals in the construction of new knowledge below, and then come back to them in following chapters. Meanwhile, some general implications can be abstracted from the work of the information processors.

KNOWLEDGE CONSTRUCTION CURRICULUM APPLICATION 6

The construction of new knowledge is controlled by an overall rational process that hinges on human goals and on previously learned metacognitive strategies. It involves complex processing of new perceptions, which are interpreted in terms of prior constructions selectively retrieved from memory. These interpretations may include sorting processes and connections to prior or brand new generalizations or algorithms. Prior constructions or schemata may or may not be accommodated or adapted to form new ones. Educational experiences need to be responsive to these processes, and educators need to understand them.

Measuring Cognitive Ability

Reflecting on the preceding, educators can assume that there is a potential for schools to provide an environment in which all kinds of abilities can develop, but we also must recognize that we are not the total culture or experience, and that therefore differences will exist in the rate at which children learn and in a measurable difference between them at the end of schooling. Preoccupation with highly constrained performance tests that measure these differences may be wasteful—perhaps even dysfunctional.

If intelligence is subject to cultural values and previous experience, and the brain is a multiple organ structure with independently operating units and performance levels, the use of specific performance tasks, with measurements such as response time to predict overall intelligence, is dead-ended by the narrowness of the tasks. Initially promising correlations of these tests with broader measurements of ability proved to be unreplicable (Lohman, 1989). This is acknowledged by Anderson (1990), who for many years employed such tasks in his intensive research on the mechanisms of cognition. After much soul searching, he ascribes the fruit-lessness of some of this work to the fact that a variety of inputs can achieve the same output—hence, the behaviors measured by these tests can not be associated with particular cognitive mechanisms in the brain.

From the practical viewpoint, speed of response may be helpful on timed tests, and of value in some life situations that require such skill, but may be valueless in determining how good the brain is at synthesizing new and previous perceptions and memory frames (pieces of knowledge or schemata stored in the brain) to help form new situation-adapted ones. Anderson (1990) posits that an elaborate memory fan (store of related or categorized declarative knowledge) may require a longer time to process and retrieve. If the brain's activity is rational and the human brain opti-mizes behavior, given different goals and environments, the speed of hu-man response may also vary.

Modular theories of intelligence also recognize that the common sense that some individuals with high measures of IQ lack may be an inde-pendently functioning set of skills and that, somewhat correspondingly, just because students cannot remember the rotely memorized steps in long division does not mean that they can not reason logically.

Based on experimental evidence, several theories recognize that there is a difference between the ability to solve problems that have been expe-rienced and the ability to solve novel problems. Experience with a prob-lem type decreases solution time. Therefore, traditional measures of in-nate intelligence or fluid ability have attempted to use novel problems to separate innate intelligence from crystallized ability. Comparative and valid measures of fluid intelligence then require us to design tasks that are equally novel to every tested individual. Can a test with such equity be constructed? Every child's experience is unique. April and Meg may use different experiences to teach the same skill. If the test question is similar to experiences that Meg has provided, it may skew the results on the test her class takes.

Anderson et al. (1996, 1997) believe that it is possible to generalize from one previously learned situation to another novel one. They posit that skill with novel problems is perhaps related to the ability to encode memory and convert it to a production or procedural rule (algorithm) that helps one find a solution. The creation of such procedural rules may be highly specific and generated only when needed because it is costly to the brain's energies (Anderson, 1990).

The difficulty in constructing generalizations may be related to the current dialogue on situated learning: a growing emphasis on the value of presenting real-life environments in schools that suggests that it is diffi-cult to transfer knowledge gained in the traditional nonrealistic environ-ments of schools to new life situations. I agree with Anderson et al. (1996, 1997) that although this is difficult, it is possible. The true value of real-life situations may be in their ability to motivate learning or control it through the rational level. Teachers can structure experiences that facilitate the production of generalizations and motivate learning.

Tying the study of human intelligence to the existing tests that differentiate individuals may have been part of the difficulty in understanding it. Recent studies of general intelligence have consequently placed a greater emphasis on how connections between parallel systems or hierarchical levels take place. These studies also recognize the importance of a knowledge base on which to build connections, and have therefore shifted from process tests to analyses of how achievement occurs, especially in such areas as mathematics and reading. The findings of these studies and those that investigate the effect of various learning environments will do much more for the schooling process than the tests that decide ahead of time, in a vacuum, who will or will not succeed. Studies of metacognitive and affective factors have already led to instructional approaches that consider the influence of thinking about learning, social goals, control, and attitude on the learning process. A preliminary discussion of the role of goals appears below. I address some of the specific analyses further in Chapter 5, "Constructing Creative Classrooms."

KNOWLEDGE CONSTRUCTION CURRICULUM APPLICATION 7

Current tests of intelligence depend on timed solutions to novel problems, and evaluate only part of an individual's abilities and potential to learn. Time for task completion may not be a valid criterion, and finding problems novel to every tested individual may be impossible. Teacher expectations of students and consequent student self-expectations should not depend on current forms of intelligence tests. It is more important to know how learning happens and the factors that affect it. Learning experiences can be connected to realistic situations, and can facilitate the creation of transferable generalizations.

Cognition, Metacognition, and Goals

The concept of a systematic connection between cognitive brain processes and controlling goals that optimize behavior sheds new light on something educators have long been aware of—the influence of students' goals on their ability to learn. This recognition adds organization and continuity to previous research on the effects of goals on achievement. It also connects what we previously considered separately as cognitive and metacognitive processes. Metacognition has been defined as being aware of thinking as one performs specific tasks, and then using this awareness to control what one is doing. The degree to which one is aware of one's thinking and knowledge as one learns or works on problems has been demonstrated to have an effect on one's ability to learn and find solutions. Sternberg's (1985) metacomponents are the conscious directors or executives of other brain processes. Generalized problem-solving skills (strategies) are examples of these.

There may be cultural differences in the way in which we use metacognitive strategies. For example, Japanese students consciously try to memorize more often than Australian students (Purdie & Hattie, 1996). Metacognition, however, also presupposes control of self, and definitions of it by some have included such affective factors as motivation, efficacy, attitude, confidence, interest, expectation, commitment, and attention (Marzano et al., 1988). These factors have been demonstrated by considerable research to be controls in the learning process.

The affective factors can be logically defined in terms of the human goals addressed by the constructivist philosophers and the cognitive researchers. As an example, consider motivation. Motivating reluctant students to want to learn is in effect changing the goals that helped govern the construction of previous realities or schemata. The athletic coach knows well the motivational power of achievement and social goals in improving performance—although some of the improvement may be physiological, much of it may be cognitive. Although human goals may sometimes be subliminal, even reflexive (such as eating without noticeable hunger), they can quickly be retrieved into consciousness and used to govern the cognitive process. A hungry hunter learns quickly how to stalk his or her prey. Understanding in a general way that human goals govern the cognitive process adds structure to the previously demonstrated relationships between effective instruction and the affective and metacognitive controlling factors.

For example, in support of the concept of goals as controls of cognitive function is the evidence that self-efficacy (e.g., Pintrich, Marx, & Boyle, 1993) is connected to knowledge acquisition. Human goals for learning are mediated by beliefs in the ability to succeed, and ultimate success by expectations thereof (e.g., Cohen & Lotan, 1995; Weinstein, Madison, & Kuklinsky, 1995). Attitudes that recognize the relationship between effort expended in the learning process and pay off have also been correlated to performance efficiency (e.g., Rogers & Saklofske, 1985). From a negative view, it can be a human goal not to care to learn or not to pay attention—especially if previous experiences have been unsuccessful or socially uncomfortable.

William Glasser (1986) describes a control theory axiom with a trench- ant metaphor in this description: "What students (and all of us) do in school (and out) is completely determined by the pictures in their heads" (p. 39). He believes that all children come to school with a picture that school is a satisfying place and are willing to work to achieve satisfaction. Lack of success changes the pictures in their heads—and their sense of power, which Glasser declares is a strong human need (and goal). Teach- ers, parents, and the peer culture help put these pictures (and goals) in children's heads. Can we be successful in changing the goals of students and get them to feel more power and achieve more? Connecting to the notion of social construction of knowledge, Urdan and Maehr (1995) de- fine goals as "the perceptions and beliefs about the purposes of academic achievement" (p. 215). They identify social goals such as "the values of whom one is affiliated with or from whom one seeks approval" (p. 221) as having possible negative or positive effects on educational outcomes. This has special bearing on the potential success of female students in science and mathematics; their present affiliations, cultural history, and tradi- tional school settings may not promote the goals required for success in these areas. Competitive environments that place a greater emphasis on speed and grades than on cooperative and realistic endeavors may be the least desirable for women, but in the long run be less productive for both male and female students (Bailey, 1996).

Interest

Interest, as another goal framer in the acquisition of new knowledge, has been studied in some depth. In a review of the literature and in his own research, Tobias (1994, 1995) relates interest and prior knowledge to each other and to the acquisition of new knowledge. Knowing something about a topic increases interest and encourages the acquisition of further knowl- edge. Tobias cites several studies that provide evidence for these relation- ships between interest and knowledge, and explains the difference be- tween situational, topic, and domain interest. He posits that situational interest can lead to broader and more sustained domain interest and pro- vides evidence that situational interest can enhance metacognitive pro- cesses such as self-monitoring. Having fun with the experience of building a robot can lead to further interest in science. It can also make you an effective robot builder.

Tobias also notes that students with low interest probably acquire much knowledge in school only because of other goals such as high grades. Such prior knowledge rarely leads to long-term retention or in- creased receptivity to related domain knowledge.

Real Experiences and Technology
in the Instructional Process

Related to situational interest is the part of Sternberg's theory that refers to the element of intelligence demonstrated in practical (relevant to life) applications (Sternberg, Okagaki, & Jackson, 1990). In addition to adding domain interest, experiences such as these may strengthen the pictures, goals, and power of students who naturally possess practical or contextual intelligence. As a result, interest in further learning may be heightened. Girls, in particular, may be positively affected by relevant to life applications, but as Bailey (1996) notes, "Although girls may be most enthusiastic about pursuing science when they see it as relevant to daily life, boys will surely not be less interested when presented with more relevance!" (p. 78).

Technological applications in the classroom greatly enlarge the possibilities for situational interest and practical applications. Even when the child interacts alone with a computer program, there is a simulation of social activity and relevant to life experience; there is immediate feedback to confirm efficacy; the child is in control and nurturing or building on a variety of intelligences. A well-done piece of software can call on metacognitive strategies. I watch my 4-year-old grandson, Edward, manipulate his mouse with *Gizmos and Gadgets* (The Learning Company, 1993, 1994), an interactive science-technology CD-ROM, and listen as he plans his strategy for building a better car. He is only on the brink of reading, but manages to identify the key words. Although he will initiate and learn alone, he prefers to have an adult or another child by his side. I have little doubt that what he learns will be generalized and transferred to new situations; I have already seen him do that!

KNOWLEDGE CONSTRUCTION CURRICULUM APPLICATION 8

Goals control learning, and therefore curriculum and learning environments must consider the effects of goals on the learning process. To be effective, teachers may need to manage student goals. Interest is a goal framer: Increased interest results in more effective knowledge construction. Real-problem situations and educational technology may heighten interest and other goals.

Connecting Research to Practice:
Summary Hypotheses

Before I summarize my hypotheses and suggest applications to the instructional process in the following chapters, it may be helpful to clarify my interpretation of the terms *schemata, connection,* and *adaptation.* Schemata or memory frames are the previously connected units stored in the brain. Connections apply to the first active phase of learning, both to the conscious adult-induced analogies and to the dynamic, multilevel, and time-ordered processing that takes place as the brain retrieves previous knowledge, matches it with goals, aligns it with newly coded input, and fits it into generalized algorithms. The adaptations of previously stored schemata are the result—the ah-ha! of new insight—and correspond to the new picture of reality described by the constructivists. The new schemata are then stored as retrievable units.

An understanding of learning as a dynamic goal-controlled social process of forming new constructions by making connections between prior knowledge, which has been informal, and new top-down formal learning experiences presents a challenge to practitioners. It suggests a method of instruction grounded in interest-high "doing" endeavors that accepts and considers the student's present knowledge, fluid and crystallized intelligence, culture, and goals, but plans for the stretching or correction of this knowledge toward what is in the social mediator's consensual domain. In conclusion, I suggest that teachers such as Meg, Brad, and April not limit their understanding to one theory, but know and consider the breadth of hypotheses and premises that have a possible influence on the construction of curriculum, and then view each situation to see how it fits. With experience, they will generalize and automatize. The suggestions in Table 3.1 are a summary based on a constructivist philosophy, which is supported by the empirically derived learning theories of cognitive psychology that also recognize the controlling influence of human goals on cognitive processes. In the chapters ahead, I refer to these hypotheses as I discuss some of the decisions teachers must make in terms of the written contracts, the enactments, and the measures of their curriculum.

TABLE 3.1   Research on Learning and the Curriculum

Theory or Finding	Inference for Curriculum Design
Each individual must construct his or her own new reality or knowledge based on connections between previous knowledge and new experiences. Individuals construct new adaptations of knowledge as a result of actions on the environment or interactions with others. They may also construct new knowledge in reflections on these actions and interactions.	The curriculum should provide experience-rich environments that promote opportunities for students to learn with understanding as active participants, rather than environments that rely on passive students and teacher telling. Technology and manipulatives should be employed to provide the richest possible active environment.
The construction of new or ever-changing adaptations of knowledge is governed by human goals.	The curriculum should pay attention to and address student goals such as affiliation, control, interest, and efficacy.
New knowledge and goals are frequently framed and modified on a social plane. New knowledge is constructed as a mediator stretches the child from previously internalized knowledge to new knowledge. The knowledge that they then share and that others may share is in the *consensual domain.*	Teachers need to plan for this stretching by carefully matching environments and planned outcomes or standards. These standards are the knowledge of the consensual domain.
The social plane may involve social artifacts (such as texts and computer programs), but is most powerful when it involves interaction, especially face-to-face human interaction.	Learning environments should provide a multitude of social artifacts and interactions such as those provided in interactive computer programs and cooperative learning.
The construction of new knowledge is enhanced in active or "doing" situations, particularly those that present high-interest novel situations.	Learning environments should provide for active participation in real-life situations and problem solving.

(continued)

TABLE 3.1 (Continued)

Theory or Finding	*Inference for Curriculum Design*
The actions and connections required in the construction of new knowledge involve several levels of brain function, including metacognitive controls and the retrieval and processing of prior knowledge.	Learning environments should provide for experiences that stimulate or connect to prior knowledge and metacognitively help the student form new algorithms or generalizations.
The individual's ability to construct new knowledge and solve problems may be a factor of the function of each of these levels of brain function, as well as a factor of the previous experience and goals.	The curriculum should respond to diagnosed differences in students' learning strategies, experience, and goals, which may have influenced their fluid and crystallized intelligence in multiple areas.
Intelligence is a multiple construct. Although some of the fluid component may be genetically predetermined or subject to physiological limits or effects, the crystallized component is responsive to environmental factors. Single measures such as IQ that rely on novel problems to compare individuals are therefore limited informers, especially because intelligence may also show variation among individuals in reference to specific skill areas.	There should be less reliance on measures that rely on speed of response and are limited in their scope to single forms of intelligence. Curriculum should provide opportunities for students to achieve satisfaction and a sense of power in their high-skill areas, but it should also stretch their lower-skill areas.
Human goals can be interpreted in terms of the affective factors such as motivation, efficacy, attitude, and interest that have previously demonstrated and recognized effects on learning.	The curriculum should consider the differences in individual and cultural goals, and provide an environment that enlists or modifies those goals toward the purpose of learning.

Notes

1. Howard Gardner's (1983, 1993,1995; see also Checkley, 1997) work has been widely disseminated both in the literature and in workshops for teachers. This scenario is based on an actual conversation I overheard at one of these workshops. Gardner's seven areas of intelligence are spatial intelligence, musical intelligence, linguistic (verbal) intelligence; logical/ mathematical intelligence, interpersonal intelligence, intrapersonal intelligence, and bodily kinesthetic intelligence. He recently added an eighth: naturalistic intelligence.

2. Although Ausubel (1963, 1968) addresses the notion that the child has to choose to learn, most of his application suggestions concern the fit into prior knowledge. He believes that the teacher needs to program that fit, and recommends the use of advance organizers, which may be a more direct form of teaching that is in contrast to the more open-ended and inductive approach suggested by constructivists.

3. An example of growing congruence between physiologists and psychologists may be the recent finding of evidence that the hippocampus of the brain functions as a connective region at the same time that psychologists using computer models suggest that new connections and adaptations of previous cognitions are the basis for new cognitive storage.

4. The algorithmic level has a significant carryover to the construction of artificial intelligence—or the ability of computers to imitate human intelligence.

4

Choosing Standards and Designing Them Down

Educators must function within the spheres of many influences: the ambient society, predetermined externally imposed standards and assessments, the parameters of their immediate school cultures, and the realities and variations of the teaching-learning process. Nevertheless, even in countries that follow uniform national standards, much is left for the school and the teacher to design. The national standards for all schooling in Japan are found in three slim volumes, the mathematics standards for fifth grade on three and a half uncrowded pages (Japanese Society of Mathematical Education, 1990)—hardly the scope of what goes on in a child's educational experience in that country.

Given the power of enacting the instructional events that make up the curriculum, therefore, teachers must make responsible and situation-bound decisions regarding these events on a daily basis with little time for analyzing their source, influences, and appropriateness. In preparation for this, teachers need to construct content designs and patterns of thinking and decision making that will facilitate their task. The creation of these designs and patterns is the process of curriculum development.

This chapter presents the "how to" stage of curriculum development. In response to these influences and new knowledge of how learning happens, how do we translate existing content fragments and the new standards into clearly articulated frameworks that are meaningful and useful to the teacher and of value to the student? Whether we are directed by national, state, professional organization, or local standards, we have to map the smaller trips on our journey toward their accomplishment, and we will want these to be on productive and rewarding paths. To do this, we need a common language for giving and reading directions, and we need to understand the way the roads feed into each other: from small individual paths for special excursions to large highways carrying us all toward the same places. How else will we know we are on the right road and how else will we know when we get there?

Consensus about the need to change and transitions from previous forms may have to come first. I therefore begin with a brief scenario of teachers engaged in the curriculum writing process that may help the reader understand the setting for this task. Then, because new constructions must be connected to prior knowledge, I review the form of the most commonly used curriculum design in schools over the past four decades and compare that with the new forms and standards-based language.

Even for experienced teachers, some of the new terminology related to standards may be strange and cumbersome. What do we mean when we use the terms *outcome, commencement standard, benchmark, content standard, performance standard,* and *enabling standard*? How do we use these terms to tell us and others what we want our students to know, understand, and be able to do? In constructing learning environments, how do we group students for instruction? How do we use the resources of time, space, materials, and human energy? What kinds of skills do students need to become better problem solvers? How can our expanding knowledge of how the brain processes and stores information guide us in the choice of experiences and interactive dialogues to help build those skills? Creating the horizontal and vertical articulations of the design is a challenge, and therefore the suggested patterns are accompanied by step-by-step templates and some criteria for evaluating the products.

The Curriculum Committee Meets

Meg was not pleased to be in the science planning group. She had not been able to attend the summer professional development workshop, but along with others had been charged with revising the school science curriculum so that it complied with new state standards. She began their first 3rd-grade group meeting with this comment, "Why don't they just tell us what else to teach—or get us a new text series that follows the standards to use with our kits?" She was perfectly happy with the science kit she was using. The kids loved playing with the magnets, lightbulbs, and batteries. It was her own enthusiasm with these materials that got her on this committee, and the thought of abandoning the kit activities made her uncomfortable.

April, on the other hand, was gung-ho for change. Her kits were rarely used because she found them cumbersome to implement. The kids messed them up and were noisy when they did the activities. She thought higher standards might put a greater emphasis on the content that was so difficult to extract from the activities. It always seemed to her that the activities were little more than play, and accomplished only minimal science. April's own background in science was not too strong, and she always felt more comfortable with a science textbook that covered the material.

Brad was enthusiastic and anxious to share what he had learned and accomplished in the summer workshop. But he was still concerned that his group of ESL students would be unfairly challenged by the rigor of the new standards and once again put down by the tests. He was apprehensive that most of the new science standards would require an emphasis on definitions, which were so difficult for his students. He had always enjoyed his own science classes, and often used a science activity to generate interest and discussion with his students. At the workshop, he had seen some new CD-ROMs with animations that were especially good for his students, who were limited in their use of the English language. Maybe this was an opportunity to meet some of their needs in a different way. "Where do we begin—these standards are so general?" he asked to initiate the discussion.

April saw an easy solution: "The advertisement for these new textbooks says that they meet the new state standards; why don't we just take a look at them and write a curriculum around the content in the text? The workbooks that supplement them are full of good stuff for the kids to do." "What about our kit activities?" Meg protested, "My students get so much out of them and science is supposed to be a process." Brad knew that reaching consensus was not going to be easy. Educational reform is not easy.

In an interesting proposal for evaluating recent educational reforms, House (1996) recommends that we examine reform suggestions in terms of three factors taken from transaction cost economic analysis; he suggests that these factors may affect the reform adoption and success rate. The first factor is *bounded rationality*, or the reality that not everyone understands everything in a rational manner. April demonstrates this in her conclusion that the new standards mean new content, easily accomplished with a new book. The second factor is *opportunism*, or the reality that people choose courses of action based on the promise of personal gain. Brad's motives may have been less selfish than this factor implies, but there is no doubt he thought this might be a good opportunity to meet his personal needs. Meg, who was not so willing to give up her successful and satisfying investment in her present science program, illustrates House's third factor. It is not easy to implement change in educational settings because teachers' already acquired skills are *asset specific* and they have already sunk time and energy in them. Meg needs to see ways to redeploy her already useful skills or be tempted by a greater reward for learning new ones.

The above scenario is a common one, often repeated in the same tone in our country's schools as teachers try to come to a consensus and comply with the call for greater uniformity in the written school curriculum. Perhaps, as a manifestation of bounded rationality, teachers who seem to have little trouble planning day-to-day activities for their students and can also state desired goals or standards in a general way have difficulty translating the generalities into more specific expectations. Aligned activities that lead toward the accomplishment of the goals are also more difficult. Choices of activities are usually loosely connected to content standards, but are frequently based on other criteria such as accessibility, student control and interest factors, and public relations appeal. For example, worksheets are easy to obtain and use; they control the children and document and advertise the curriculum to a parent and supervisory audience. This makes them asset specific (and comfortable) investments. By design, they mimic the standardized tests used as measures of our own performance as well as the children's, and are therefore opportunistic.

A Bit of History

In consideration of House's (1996) principles, before we suggest a different way to organize curriculum, it may be useful to avoid some bounded rationality by examining our already comfortable asset specific investment: the history and substance of current curriculum forms. We then may be able to illustrate how making the required changes in forms and substance can prove opportunistic in its potential benefit to teachers and learners.

Many of us attribute traditional organization of the curriculum and usage of the terms *goals* and *objectives* to curriculum theorist Ralph Tyler (1949). For most of the latter half of this century, written school curriculums were organized into related and hierarchical units that described the scope of what children were expected to learn. They not only described the breadth of this knowledge and suggested experiences, but also were often explicit about what was to be covered at each grade level. Broader goals and their related more specific objectives could be stated in terms of either the *giver* or the *receiver*. A giver objective or aim might be "Students will be required to read one Shakespearean play in the 10th grade." If the objective described what the student or receiver would be able to do, it was a behavioral objective such as "Students will be able to discuss Hamlet's state of mind."

In their most expanded form, behavioral objectives that were designed to lead to the accomplishment of the goals also had specific levels of performance attached to them. These behavioral objectives were sometimes so isolated and focused on a specific behavior, such as "Students will correctly identify the forms of the verb 'to be' with 80% accuracy," that teachers found them cumbersome, confining, and detached from the original broader goals. In addition, attempts in the 1960s and 1970s to attach behavioral objectives to extensive designs for individualization of instruction dampened teachers' and students' enthusiasm as classroom activities deteriorated into the tons of ditto sheets that made up the "learning activity packages." Teachers soon were bogged down in grading papers and the management of many students doing many different things. The social interactions and group processes that motivated both teachers and students were missing from this scheme; their human, adaptive interventions were undermined by this process. As a consequence of the resulting diminution of interest in individualized instruction and a countercurrent of cooperative learning in the 1990s, there is less focus on behavioral objectives, but much of our curriculum and assessments still bears this organization. The recent use of computers to manage independent activity has kept this approach alive.

American individualism and the prevailing spirit of local control of education have worked to prevent the organizational form of written curriculum as goals and objectives from providing much in the way of consistency from school to school or state to state. The design was never meant to be a prescription for a nationwide curriculum. Instead, there were many adaptations and variations. These official written curriculums of individual schools were also frequently unaligned with the actual curriculum as enacted in the classroom. Any degree of consistency was more likely to be attained by commercial textbooks and standardized tests.

In an attempt to place more emphasis on broader, more meaningful, but measurable outcomes—always focused on the receiver—the outcomes-based movement of the late 1980s gained rapid interest and favor. The curriculum of several communities and states was reorganized around exit or commencement outcomes that were then "designed down," or articulated with benchmarks at critical grade levels and finally with grade-level or unit outcomes. Common to all well-structured examples of units of curriculum design is a design-down element that articulates the general with the more specific so that the smaller curriculum fragments will lead toward the accomplishment of the broader desired ends. Outcomes were to be carefully matched to assessments, with a focus on the more "authentic" performances (Spady & Marshall, 1990).

Unfortunately, as reported in Chapter 1, "Weren't There Always Curriculum Standards?" just as the outcomes-based education effort was gaining national momentum in the early 1990s, it suddenly was met by grassroots opposition from conservative groups that objected to some of the values-oriented outcomes and the concept that everyone be held accountable for the same goals. Quickly, the term *standard* replaced *outcome* in the educational literature and governmental plans. The change was accelerated by the new term's more politically palatable connotation of traditional excellence. The concept of an articulated designed-down curriculum, however, transfers easily to the new terminology.

Defining Standards in New Terms

Evidence of the remarkable political power of the concept of higher standards is clearly embedded in current national calls for action on raising education standards at both the state and federal levels. As they have been developed by some individual states and professional organizations such as the National Council of Teachers of Mathematics and the New Standards Program (a coalition of the Learning and Research Development Center and the National Center on Education and the Economy), standards are essentially outcomes or receiver-based objectives that may or may not have attached performance measures. They retain the design-down potential of outcomes-based instruction but differ in their intent from goals and objectives in that they are prescriptions designed for the purpose of higher expectations and uniformity.

As outlined in the tables in this chapter, in many respects the standards parallel traditional goals and objectives as well as outcomes. But they have been more specifically organized (by McREL, 1993, and others) into content standards, performance standards, and variably into curriculum or opportunity-to-learn standards. For the National Education Summit in 1996, Borthwick and Nolan (1996, p. 1) defined the terms as follows: Content standards "provide guidance for the design of instructional programs" and "a tool for checking the quality . . . in terms of coverage of expected knowledge and skills. Content standards tell us what we want our students to know and what we want them to be able to do." But they are "limited in their ability to improve student achievement because they do not tackle the crucial question of performance." Aligned performance measures are therefore necessary. These, which contain specific performance indicators and performance tasks, more clearly describe "how good is good enough" and are termed *performance standards* (Council for Basic Education, 1996; McREL, 1993). When constructed, the performance standards should be reflections of the content standards they measure. An analogy that might help is to compare them to two sides of a hand. The back of the hand defines its form and its potential, but the palm is the implement and measure of what it does.

Curriculum Enactment

Curriculum, in its current interpretation, implies the total school experience. Content standards represent a kind of planned vision for the desired results of the curriculum, and performance standards represent a design for measuring these results. Neither of these addresses the many other variables that affect what happens in schools: the day-to-day variations in students, teachers, and the classroom environment that more closely frame the enacted curriculum (Ball & Cohen, 1996). They are a destination without a road map. In Weinstein, Madison, and Kuklinsky's (1996) words, "Simply willing higher expectations without attention to effective teaching practices will not result in higher achievement" (p. 16).

The enacted curriculum is what ultimately affects student achievement, and it requires the equal attention of standards. Although standards attached to the variables of the enacted curriculum have been defined as curriculum standards or opportunity-to-learn standards (Council for Basic Education, 1996; McREL, 1993), this may be confusing terminology. The term *curriculum* in its modern interpretation is broad and includes all the facets of instructional delivery. Opportunity to learn has socially positive implications, but the term *enabling standards* may be a better choice. This borrows from the historical use of the term *enabling objectives*, which refers to the activities that support the desired goals and objectives. Extending the historical use of the term to the concept of standards, enabling standards address the conditions of the school environment, or as I refer to it in Chapter 5, "Constructing Creative Classrooms," the setting. The specifics of the experience, discourse, and actions with materials that the student is engaged in are then the *enabling activities*.

To help summarize the above definitions, Table 4.1 compares the current terminology of content and performance standards with the historic use of goals and objectives. Table 4.2 illustrates the very important design down or vertical articulation process, and Table 4.3 illustrates the horizontal articulation of content, performance, and enabling standards. A general standard such as "students will be good problem solvers" can be met at many different levels and in the context of different content areas.

The upside down tree in Figure 4.1 illustrates the design-down and delivery process. The tree is shown upside down because the design is the beginning, and we think of the processes as "design down" and "deliver up." Like the trunk of a tree, the general standards support a widely reaching set of branches and leaves. Curriculum is designed down from the more general commencement or exit level to the more specific benchmark level, and then to the even more specific level of the course, grade, and unit. But just as the leaves in turn must manufacture food and nurture the trunk, the more specific designed-down content standards must feed the general ones—they deliver up and make the general ones happen. None of this works if the connections of internal flow are impeded. The junctures where twigs meet branches and branches meet trunks are particularly important. The outcome of each lesson of the leaves is fed through a twig to the branch that is the unit, and then into a larger one that is the grade level. Several grade levels may feed into a larger branch at a benchmark juncture, and this, in turn, finally meets the main trunk.

TABLE 4.1 Comparing Traditional Goals and Objectives With Standards

Goals and Objectives	Standards
☛ **Overall goals** are general statements of the broader intents of the educational process. They may be stated for large groups of students at varying levels or for smaller groups at specific levels. They usually are neither specific nor suggest any action or measures.	☛ **Commencement-level standards** resemble goals in their generality, but describe the individual's capability at a specific terminal education point such as high school graduation. They may or may not have attached performance measures.
☛ **Objectives** are designed down from **goals.** Objectives may focus on the giver or the receiver: On the giver: *To prepare students to be good citizens.* On the receiver (behavioral objective) *Students will be able to make decisions that are good for society.*	☛ **Benchmark-level standards** are designed down from **exit or commencement-level standards. Grade-level or course standards or outcomes** are designed down from benchmark standards. Standards focus on the receiver—although the receiver may be a group such as a school. *Students will become good citizens.* *Students will be able to make decisions that are good for society.* *The school will prepare students for the technological future.*
☛ Goals and objectives may be described in terms of a description of self, or in terms of conceptual or procedural knowledge. **Conceptual knowledge** objectives answer the question "What should students know?" For example: *Students will know that selective burning is an effective measure for controlling forest fires.* **Procedural knowledge** objectives answer the question, "What should students be able to do?" For example: *Students will be able to prevent forest fires.*	☛ Standards may be described in terms of a description of self, or in terms of conceptual or procedural knowledge. **Conceptual knowledge** standards answer the question: "What should students know?" For example: *Students will know that selective burning is an effective measure for controlling forest fires.* **Procedural knowledge** standards answer the question: "What should students be able to do?" For example: *Students will be able to prevent forest fires.* Conceptual and procedural knowledge standards that do not have specific performance measures (such as those below) are **content standards.**
☛ **Behavioral objectives** may or may not have a level of performance stated; if they do they are performance based. For example: *Students will be able to choose environmentally sound actions from a list with 80% accuracy.*	☛ If standards do have specific performance indicators and performance tasks, they are **performance standards.** For example: *Given a written problem situation, students will be able to describe three measures that prevent forest fires.*
☛ **Goals and objectives are planning guides.**	☛ **Standards are prescriptions for creating uniformity.**

TABLE 4.2 Designing Down from Commencement Standards to Benchmarks and Courses: Some Vertical Articulation Examples

---

Commencement Content Standard: Students Will Be Good Problem Solvers

---

- Benchmark Level 1 (6th grade): Content standard

Students will understand and apply skills related to gathering, evaluating, interpreting, and presenting information.

> Fourth grade content standard: *Students will know how to make a bar graph from data.*

> Matching fourth grade performance standard: *Students will correctly record a set of temperature data and translate it to a bar graph*

- Benchmark Level 2 (10th grade): Content standard

Students will use formal and informal reasoning processes in applying problem-solving, decision-making, and negotiating techniques.

> Algebra course content standard: *Students will know how logarithms are related to our base-10 number system.*

> Matching algebra course performance standard: *Students will explain how a logarithm is determined and apply this to the structure and derivation of a table of logarithms.*

Commencement Content Standard: Students Will Be Good Communicators

---

- Benchmark Level 1 (6th grade): Content standard

Students will be able to communicate their thoughts and ideas in written form.

> 4th grade content standard: *Students will know that a good topic sentence provides focus for a paragraph.*

> Matching 4th grade performance standard: *Students will write a book report that has topic sentences that provide four paragraphs with good focus.*

- Benchmark Level 2 (10th grade): Content standard

Students will understand the forms, techniques, and stylistic requirements of a variety of written communications.

> 9th grade content standard: *Students will be able to write a persuasive essay.*

> Matching 9th grade performance standard: *Students will write a persuasive essay that clearly delineates a point of view and provides at least three reasons to support it.*

TABLE 4.3 Horizontal Articulation Examples of Standards

Content Standards	Performance Standards	Enabling Standards
At grade 1, students will know that addition is an increase on the number line, subtraction is a decrease in the number line, and there are symbols (+) and (-) for the operations.	*At grade 1*, students will be able to provide the correct new number by counting on a number line, when solving change/result unknown addition problems that simulate their own prior or present experience.	*Grade 1* teachers will understand the sequence of the way research has told us students learn to add and subtract: from the changes on a number line to counting on and down from the first number to the more complex choices and interpretations of noncanonical problems.
At grade 2, students will know that: addition (+) is a combining of parts to form a whole and subtraction (-) is a separation from the whole, and that the parts and whole can be represented by number symbols representing the real amounts (referents).	*At grade 2*, students will compute the correct new number by counting on (adding) from the first number or counting down (subtracting) from the first number, in change/result unknown problems, combine problems, and part unknown problems based on their own present or prior experience.	*Grade 2* teachers will structure appropriate problems and dialogue, diagnose student misconceptions and use the necessary materials. Each *grade 2* student will have at least one uninterrupted hour for math each day; including some early morning time. Group problem solving with peer interaction will be integrated into every math lesson and supersede time spent on computation practice.
Students will have achieved the cardinal principle (see quantities as units) and not have to count all.	Students will identify the unit parts and whole in canonical and noncanonical problem forms.	
		Classrooms will be provided with interactive technology and manipulative materials such as unifix cubes and bead frames.

At the same time, there must be horizontal articulation. As the leaves turn toward the sun, the carbon dioxide must enter them. The performance standards must match the content standards and measure achievement. When based on carefully reviewed previous experience, the settings and activities of well-planned enabling standards can have a reasonable

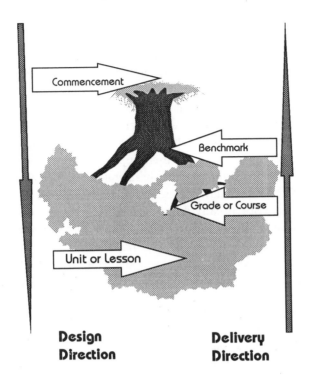

Figure 4.1. Curriculum Planning

probability for helping the student be successful in these measures. They should encompass a wider scope of the variables of the classroom experience: the teachers' knowledge, the discourse, the materials, the allocation of time and space, the social contexts of peers and adults. Attention to a comprehensive design process can bring some needed coherence and clarity to planned school curriculums. However, the achievement of greater equity in the enacted curriculum for all students is a far greater challenge. The preplanned design is only the first step.

A comparison sample of some very specific and matched standards of each type appears in Table 4.3. The listed standards—especially the enabling ones—are not meant to be all-inclusive. The enabling activities should entail the greatest flexibility and choice. With consistency in the content and performance standards as the objective, and reasonable equity in the enabling standards, teachers can be creative, responsive, and timely with the specifics of day-to-day activities. Tables 4.1, 4.2, and 4.3 are merely illustrations of possible articulations. I address the specifics of performance and enabling standards in greater detail in following chapters.

Getting Started on Planning Curriculum

Most of the standards being produced by the states and by national professional groups are very general. This gives the local school and individual teacher both the freedom and the responsibility to provide the specifics. This is as it should be, because unless teachers are directly involved in writing or choosing standards, their ownership in them will be diminished and their implementation encumbered (Solomon, 1995). Meg, April, and Brad need to understand this and then approach their task from a pragmatic point of view. Instead of feeling threatened by the charge to plan curriculum that addresses the new standards, they might seize this opportunity to revisit what they are already doing and see how it does or does not fit.

There are a number of criteria to consider to determine the goodness of fit of the present program. Does it work to accomplish any mandated standards? Does it work to meet the social and motivational goals of the students such as personal self-efficacy? Does it work for the teachers, giving them a sense of accomplishment and intrinsic reward? Does recent research on how learning takes place and constructivist theory, which states that each individual must construct his or her own knowledge, explain why it may or may not be effective?

In considering the enabling standards and activities and the ultimate enactment of the curriculum, teachers may also consider some new alternatives that have been tried elsewhere. Current technology allows us unprecedented access to the work of others. The Internet is an astounding resource, but each situation is different; each population of students and the expectations of the community from which they come is different; the parameters of time and space are different. New alternatives must be carefully approached with the same and additional questions. What kind of additional outside help will we need to implement this new program? Will we be discarding something that is asset specific to us (House, 1996), something we do not wish to discard? Too often, educators blindly buy into a new cleverly packaged program that we do not truly understand or that has little application for our current situation and needs.

If the present trend continues, teachers engaged in curriculum construction will probably have to confront and address the general standards that have already been decided at a state, city, district, or professional organization level. These will require interpretation and specificity if they are to be of any value as a guide for teaching and learning.

A Template for Action

A good way for April, Meg, and Brad to get started on planning their new curriculum is to begin, as I did, with a first-stage review of current knowledge of how learning takes place. Then they must ask themselves some simple questions that will further diminish their bounded rationality and help them bring clarity to the task. An analysis of mandated standards comes first:

- What specific things do these standards require our students to know?
- What specific things do they require our students to be able to do?
- How will these standards be measured?
- What will be the consequences of poor performance on these measures?

Next, they might consider the feasibility of the task and the circumstances with which they will have to deal. These questions need to be answered:

- What is our students' present level of development? What are they ready for?
- Which of these standards (and what others) can we help them achieve?
- What is our students' present level of knowledge? What do they already know?
- How will our students' cultural differences, goals, and interests affect their ability to achieve the standards?
- What are our own resources of time (schedules, etc.), space, human energies, and materials? How much allotted time and space can we use for this purpose, and how can we make some necessary adjustments? What other new resources will be available to us, such as new technology, books, manipulative materials, teacher assistant time?

April, Meg, and Brad may need help from experts and colleagues who have already tackled the task. I address the potential for this in Chapter 7, "Where Do We Go From Here?" Nevertheless, they should not forget the support they can give each other:

- How can we share the effort, the acquisition of resources and knowledge, the risks?

The answers to these questions and decisions made in response to them form the framework for decisions about content standards. The consequences that may be attached to matching performance standards may leave little choice or opportunity to be creative with the content standards. But as educators review these and simultaneously structure their enabling standards, greater clarity and ways to adapt may be uncovered. If team teaching is a necessary time or space parameter to accomplish the new content standard, then that becomes an enabling standard. If Meg, April, and Brad believe that an outdoor experience is necessary to accomplish the new content standard of knowing how organisms interact with each other, and the ability to identify three different animal habitats in an outdoor setting is a performance standard, then the outdoor experience becomes an enabling standard. Teachers in an inner-city system may have some difficulty with that enabling standard, but if it is understood as necessary, adjustments will have to be made—not, one hopes, in the content standard.

In the second stage, educators can design their own matched performance measures for each standard and carefully evaluate those that are mandated. They should answer the questions, How will we know when students get there? and How good is good enough? They also need to address such subquestions as:

- How reliable and valid are the measures?

- Are the assessments equitable in terms of the variations among my students?

- How easy are the assessments to administer?

- How meaningful are the interpretations: to the parents, to the students, to the public?

- What is the value to the child of the assessment experience?

The answers to these questions are the beginning framework for performance standards. The specifics of assessment and the planning for enabling standards and activities that constitute stage 3 are addressed in the following chapters, but the process of specifically clarifying expectations and measures is in itself a worthwhile endeavor. For example, a traditional statement of a science objective or standard might be "Students will know the parts of a cell and their functions," but the parts a teacher may wish 6th graders to know are probably very different from the parts and functions a teacher wishes a 10th grader to know. The measure of how well they know these parts will be different. A well-stated content standard is more explicit about what parts, and a well-constructed performance standard describes exactly how to tell whether students know them. This may bring much greater clarity to some of the present curriculum fuzziness that sometimes exists.

If the task of adding explicit clarity to the standards is shared among teachers with common responsibilities, there is the greater advantage of social construction of new knowledge and the sharing of risks. Reaching consensus on everything may be difficult, however, and absolute equity of resources may be unattainable. Individual alternatives for enabling activities may need to be considered. If they do not compromise the equity of expectation of all students in reference to the content standards, individual alternatives should not be discouraged. Teachers need to meet their

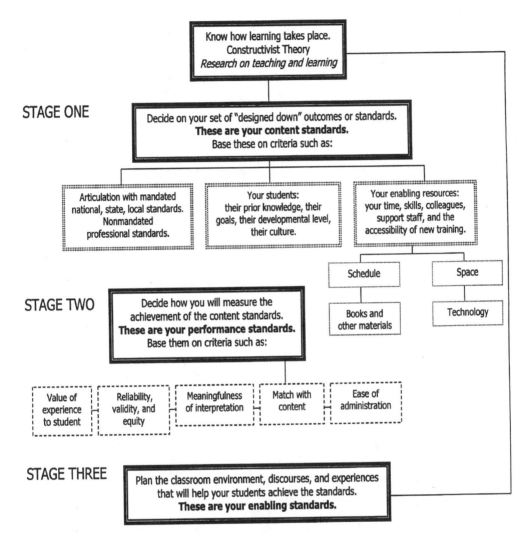

Figure 4.2. Building a Standards-Based Curriculum

own needs for creativity and individuality, and the disparities of students, cultures, and learning environments require flexibility.

Figure 4.2 organizes the steps listed above in graphic form. As work for each content standard progresses, it is useful to stop and reflect on some more specific criteria for assessing the quality of the proposed standards. Table 4.4 and Tables 5.1 and 6.1 contain some recommendations based on previous discussions of current educational research, public agendas, and the suggestions of the in-service teachers with whom I work. These are by no means all-inclusive. Individual teams and individual teachers should add their own criteria. Students themselves can offer good suggestions for what they may need and what will work for them.

Once curriculum is documented, it becomes a contract, an agreement to try to achieve what has been decided on. Although this contract re-

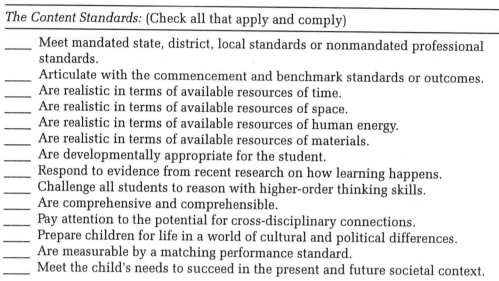

TABLE 4.4 Sample Criteria for Evaluating the Content Standards of a Grade-Level Curriculum

The Content Standards: (Check all that apply and comply)

_____ Meet mandated state, district, local standards or nonmandated professional standards.

_____ Articulate with the commencement and benchmark standards or outcomes.

_____ Are realistic in terms of available resources of time.

_____ Are realistic in terms of available resources of space.

_____ Are realistic in terms of available resources of human energy.

_____ Are realistic in terms of available resources of materials.

_____ Are developmentally appropriate for the student.

_____ Respond to evidence from recent research on how learning happens.

_____ Challenge all students to reason with higher-order thinking skills.

_____ Are comprehensive and comprehensible.

_____ Pay attention to the potential for cross-disciplinary connections.

_____ Prepare children for life in a world of cultural and political differences.

_____ Are measurable by a matching performance standard.

_____ Meet the child's needs to succeed in the present and future societal context.

quires respect and compliance, it should never be cast in stone. The curriculum has to be able to respond to the many variables of human interactions in a classroom. Most of this flexibility should be in the enabling activities. Teachers need to be free to try new approaches to reaching the common content standards. The timeliness of curriculum is also a factor that requires flexibility. Two years ago, I made entreaties to my students to learn to use the searching capabilities of library computer networks. This year, I cautioned them to be careful and critical of the unjuried publications on the Internet. Two years ago, my favorite suggested math problems for 4th graders involved Power Rangers; these suggestions would turn kids off today. *Nintendo 64* games would be better bet.

It takes time for change to happen. In spite of the greater availability of ever-changing technology, some teachers are not yet comfortable with it. They may need time and other professional development resources to develop their own skills, and adjustments in the enabling standards may have to be made. Meg, April, and Brad may feel imposed on by the external pressures of power and control that have energized this latest (and perhaps misinformed) public effort to improve our schools by setting common standards. They can seize this timely opportunity, however, to make the new standards work for them. The process of analyzing what they are now doing in reference to the more organized and ultimate purposes called for in the standards may help them focus together on a new and better way—or convince them that what they are already doing is just fine. But the task should never really end. It requires constant reflection and adjustment, and support from all who care.

5

Constructing Creative Classrooms

Meg was determined to find some justification for adding the science kit activities she had previously enjoyed to the new curriculum. She searched her closet for the state curriculum guide she remembered storing, but rarely referred to. It was never mandated, and there was no test in science at her grade. She had always more or less followed the directions in the kits she had ordered from a commercial supply company. There were some sections in a science textbook that she had students read from time to time, but these seemed unrelated to the kits. The students also produced some interesting things for the annual school science fair, but Meg always felt that the competition was unfair to students whose parents couldn't help.

Basic curriculum has not traditionally been prescribed in most states, merely recommended.[1] In New York, for example, long before the new standards were generated, state and local curriculum documents were written, disseminated, and updated from time to time by state employees working with teacher committees. Nevertheless, with the exception of high school regents courses, where the assessments are specifically based on the content of the written documents, the formal objectives of written curriculums were often ignored by classroom teachers (Ball & Cohen, 1996).

This disparity between written and enacted curriculum has been attributed to several factors, including the lack of preparation of teachers to teach in new ways, their own individualistic need to be creative, and their imperative to respond to the individual needs of students (Sarason, 1983,

1990; Solomon, 1995). Even when curriculums are developed and contracted by teams of user teachers, they are often not consulted and left to collect dust on closet shelves—unless they are rich in the details of suggested student experiences and materials. Meg and her colleagues tended to focus more on the activities and less on specific desired ends. Good activities and materials were what Meg needed to make her day successful. She assumed that if these worked with her students, in the long run and over time, the outcomes or objectives in the written curriculum would come automatically. And, based on previous records of success, this did happen often—but not all the time.

Activities and materials are the stuff of classroom environments, the everyday plans and teacher choices. Unfortunately, these choices are sometimes based on factors such as habits and comforts of practice, student control, teacher interest and comfort, and the availability of the materials and other resources instead of on how well the materials will accomplish a particular desired outcome. The choices teachers make may also be constrained by forces outside their control, such as school schedules and grouping or tracking policies.

The ultimate expectation of the educational reformers who insist on higher standards for the students of this nation is that written and agreed-on standards will have a positive effect on educational outcomes. This belief is based on the assumption that the problems of some groups of students are caused by a lack of equity in expectations. But these expectations in their written standards form will again collect dust on a closet shelf if the environment that is created for every child does not enable learning to happen. It is the possibility of equity in the enabling standards that offers the educational community the greatest promise for improvement in its endeavors. In this chapter, I address these standards of the environment and the enabling activities that energize them.

Organizing the Environment

Teaching has frequently been described as performance. Perhaps, it may be useful to take the students out of the audience, place them into the action as performers, and then continue the metaphor by adding the other elements of effective drama. The ultimate theater of the school environment revolves around three pivots: the setting and its props, the actors (including the student-performers and the teacher-director), and the dialogue and movements of the script. If everything works when the classroom curtain is raised, we may have an educational hit.

Included in the instructional setting are factors that research has related to the rate of learning, such as student group formations (including those of tracking and cooperative learning), the use of time and space, the props of materials and technology, and other classroom management elements. The effectiveness of the setting on the performance of the actors hinges on many other components. The student-performers must be engaged, alerted to new perceptions, connected to prior experience, and driven by personal and social goals that enhance rather than deter the knowledge construction process. The teacher-director must have outcomes in mind, but be open to and ready to seize on the unexpected ones. Expectations and directions need to be communicated with clarity. The varying talents, personalities, skills, and prior experiences of the actors must be considered and incorporated into both group and individual plans for new growth, adaptations, or corrections.

The dialogue and physical interactions of the script are critical. Not just the words count, but who speaks to whom in what form and with what emphasis. The position and nonverbal signals of the performers and director are significant. The script elements also include scaffolding the stretch across the zone of proximal development, or as Steffe and D'Ambrosio (1995) have redefined it, the *zone of potential construction;* directing and creating new perceptions; assessing and stimulating prior knowledge; nurturing and adapting goals; and suggesting metacognitive strategies.

Each of these pivots of the theater of school learning is discussed below with reference to how they connect to the knowledge of how learning takes place, and is accompanied by specific suggestions for creating productive environments.

The Setting

Organizing Groups of Students

A recent announcement by Rudy Crew, the chancellor of New York City schools, was greeted with mixed reaction (Steinberg, 1997). Dr. Crew recommended that new criteria and procedures be instituted for placing students in the city's program for gifted students. He was particularly concerned that reliance on traditional IQ tests, sometimes paid for by parents, eliminated the potential participation of talented minority students. Programs for gifted students are highly subject to the influences of parents, often with the support of other political entities and the entrenched beliefs of school personnel (see Wells, Hirschberg, Lipton, & Oakes, 1995). Similar influences are exerted by some groups of parents of students who have been identified as having minor learning disabilities and in need of special education.

Homogeneous grouping of students based on ability or achievement can be accomplished in several different forms. The major dichotomy is interclass grouping, in which large groups of students are tracked into special classes, and within-class grouping, in which groups are formed within a class based on differential abilities. Traditional reading groups are an example of the latter. There are also variations, such as regrouping of students among teams of classes for different subjects. Within-class homogeneous grouping is much less politically volatile, and has been suggested as an alternative for the spiraling growth of special education classes.

The research evidence on the effectiveness of both kinds of grouping is mixed. In multianalytic studies, Slavin (1987, 1990) found little academic gain but no detriment for students grouped for the full day into homogeneous groups, but he does not recommend such grouping. Instead, he suggests various homogeneous within-class groups. Kulik (cited in Allan, 1991) found, in contrast, that there was an advantage for high-ability students in whole-class homogeneous settings, somewhat less of an advantage for middle-ability students, and none for low-ability students.

In a more recent review of the effects of within-class groupings, Lou et al. (1996) studied 145 research reports and discovered that, whereas middle-level students gained the most from homogeneous groupings, lower-level students benefited most from heterogeneous groups, and higher-level students showed no significant difference between their performance in the two group forms. In addition to the important overall discovery that achievement is significantly greater in classes organized into small groups than it is in classes instructed in whole class groups, Lou et al. found other interesting affecting group factors. The level of teacher training, the size of the groups, and the subject matter make a difference. As would be expected, better teacher preparation increases the positive effects of organizing students into small groups, and smaller size groups of three or four students are more effective than larger groups. Math and science benefit more from small group work than reading and language arts—perhaps because they have the added component of problem solving. And in an unsurprising and much-supported finding, Lou et al. conclude that small groups accompanied by the cooperative learning element of structured interdependence between group members are the most effective (e.g., Johnson & Johnson, 1989; Qin, Johnson, & Johnson, 1995).

Connections to our understanding of how learning takes place explain these findings. From the goal and control perspective, the small group setting nurtures the human need for control of the learning process; interactive dialogue and time and movement adjustments are easier and more frequent. Small groups proffer satisfaction of the social goal of peer affinity (the group needs to learn this and I belong to it). They provide more opportunities for achieving a sense of self-efficacy (there are more chances for venturing an answer and there is less risk for a wrong answer). They have the advantage of sharing metacognitive strategies and receiving reminders and corrections from peers as the group proceeds—especially if the context is one of problem solving.

From the cognitive perspective, there are increases in perceptions from the interactive dialogue and greater opportunities for students to experience disequilibrium, discrepant events, or dissatisfaction with currently held constructs that will prepare them to revise, enlarge, or correct these constructs. There are mediating peers to scaffold the stretch across the zone of potential construction, and freedom for students to think out loud as they construct new knowledge.

For students grouped in lower-level homogeneous groups, these advantages may be diminished. They lose the advantage of scaffolding by more capable students, especially if these students are responsible for this—and there is evidence that higher-ability students ask more complex questions. Certainly, the label of being in the lower group may decrease feelings of self-esteem. Higher-level students in heterogeneous groups may lose some of the advantage of having the more challenging and complex questions of additional high-level students, but this may be overridden by the greater feeling of efficacy and the cognitive advantage of having to communicate constructs to others (the best way to learn something is to teach it).

I distinctly remember that my own children had less-than-accurate self-concepts when they were placed in highly competitive homogeneous groups of high achievers and did not end at the top of the class. It was only when they had the opportunity to compare themselves with the real world that these self-concepts became more realistic. In consideration of the above, I offer the following suggestion for enabling standards.

SUGGESTION FOR STANDARDS AND ENABLING ACTIVITIES

Enabling standards and activities that include a heterogeneous classroom organized into within-class small groups that have both individual accountability and interdependence are desirable because they increase the potential to accomplish content and performance standards. Moreover, the content and performance standards themselves may need to include the skills necessary for collaborative effort.

Allocations of Time

The research base that would provide a firm rationale for deciding enabling standards of time and space is very slim, but schools have been sensitive to its influence and responded. In a previous publication on the role of time in effecting school change (Solomon, 1995), I defined time in three perspectives: as a resource, in its passage, and in its sense of timeliness. It may be useful to pursue these perspectives here as well. In respect to time as a resource for learning, a well-circulated government publication called *Prisoners of Time* (National Education Commission on Time and Learning, 1994) outlines how schools are constrained by the inherited schedules of an agrarian society, and illustrates how little time is allocated to actual instruction. Although it is difficult to manage changes in structures that are firmly entrenched in our national culture, some schools are attempting to increase allocated time by experimenting with radically different calendars such as the 12-month school year. Until such changes are widespread, plans and specifications for the best use of allocated time may be a critical part of the enabling standards.

Allocated time is itself subject to the actual engagement or attention of the student to the task that is designed to help construct knowledge. The attention of students within planned activities is discussed in the sections below in reference to the management of goals and dialogue, but school routines and time schedules are external variables that can be adjusted to guarantee that interruptions in the enabling activities are at a minimum. Elementary schools have tried inviolate time periods when no students are pulled out for special classes and all interschool messages are withheld in an attempt to maintain momentum and maximize allocated time. Interruptive low-priority activities that have little effect on learning can also be evaluated and made more efficient or eliminated (Saphier & Gower, 1997).

At the secondary level, a major difficulty has been the disruptive nature of short time periods and the constant movement of students from one place and subject to another. In response, innovative middle school schedules with 4 longer period days in a 6-day schedule and class sequences where concept development classes are followed by individual progress groups have proven successful (Canady & Rettig, 1995). High schools have tackled the time problem with longer blocks of time that treat fewer subject classes in a single day, but cover all the content subjects by the end of a trimester school year (Edwards, 1995; Stumpf, 1995).

There is no doubt that spending more uninterrupted and engaged time on teacher- or peer-mediated learning activities will increase the rate of construction of the knowledge expected by the new standards, but one must also consider time from the perspective of its passage. Students develop over time; they may not be ready to add new perceptions or discard old ones. Some students need more time than others to make new constructions. The stretch across the zone of potential construction may have to occur in small increments. The enabling standards must recognize and provide for these variations.

Timeliness is another factor to consider. Receptivity to the acquisition of new knowledge varies over the school day. For the brain to work at its optimum in processing new perceptions and adapting prior constructs, it must be well nourished, untired, and uncluttered. Elementary teachers have always recognized this, and because they usually consider reading as their highest priority, they teach that in the early morning. If students are expected to reach higher standards in math, then the allocation of some of that early morning time may have to become an enabling standard.

The effectiveness of enabling activity choices may also be governed by timeliness and its connected cultural relevance. The occurrence of a startling weather phenomenon is the best time to study weather. The Olympic events are a good time to study the history of Greece or its influence on our culture. A presidential election is the time to consider our democratic processes, the statistical processes in poll taking, or the power of the written or spoken words of the media. Teachers have always capitalized on such high-interest events. Situational interest is a motivating goal that positively mitigates the cognitive process.

In contrast, anachronistic and culturally irrelevant connections can be dysfunctional. Children's goals change rapidly in response to their own development and cultural influences. Their culture is more than the home environment; it is their peers, the latest TV commercial or show or Disney film, or for teenagers, the latest pop CD, movie star, or athlete. The Power Ranger toys that were excellent foil for math problems and reading activities a few years ago wouldn't work today, but Star Wars applications and Stine horror books might. Timeliness, in respect to the receptivity of students at a particular stage of development and within their current culture, is one of the many reasons why teachers should have flexibility in the creation of enabling activities—and another reason why quickly outdated and externally designed curriculum materials packages do not always work.

SUGGESTION FOR STANDARDS AND ENABLING ACTIVITIES

Adequate, engaged, uninterrupted, and high-energy time must be provided and guarded. Students need some flexibility in the time it takes to achieve standards. Performance standards should reflect these differences. Enabling activities should be developmentally appropriate, timely, and responsive to the changing culture, student goals, and interest.

Allocations of Space and Place

The concept of open schools and classrooms had a brief period of enthusiasm in the 1960s. Schools were built without walls between classrooms and with open shared spaces. The theory behind this was that openness would provide students and teachers with greater flexibility and freedom in their learning space. Classrooms would change from the pattern of a single teacher in front of the whole class into a more student-centered learning environment. Unfortunately, the teaching methods did not change with the change in environment, and teachers in these new settings attempted to teach in their ordinary teacher-directed and isolated way. They suffered feelings of anxiety and frustration with the lack of privacy and the increased distractions of their colleagues' classes. Teacher-to-teacher peer relationships sometimes deteriorated.

Flexible arrangements of space are necessary for classrooms that nurture students' needs for autonomy and support their differing intelligences and learning styles. Some children need to have a private and undistracted space in which to study. The need for privacy may itself be a controlling human goal, and some students may require the diminished distractions of a private place to process new perceptions. I remember one particular classroom with a study loft that was a favorite place for students to retreat with a book to read or for small groups to prepare a presentation in private. A similar loft for small group work that doubles as a puppet theater is described by George (1995). Arrangements of classroom space into activity centers that challenge the many senses and allow for student choices have been effectively used for a number of years because they are congruent with cognitive processing and preemptive goal management.

If content and performance standards call for students to work on teams, to assume greater responsibility for their own learning, and to have the ability to apply knowledge to the real situations of our rapidly changing technological society, the spaces of the traditional classroom may not work. If the promises of educational technology are to be realized, technology must be accessible to every child. Cooperative learning requires spaces for groups to work with face-to-face interaction. Research centers and demonstration preparation centers will be necessary to meet the more authentic performance indicators (see Chapter 6, "How Are We Doing? Measuring Success"). The provision of instructionally functional space has become a critical enabling standard.

In some cases, it may be advantageous to move outside the classroom into other spaces to create the appropriate setting. There is no better place to study the environment than in an outdoor setting. A recent visit to a Challenger Space Center had me and a group of 5th graders in awe. We were transported in separate groups into the control center and into the spaceship. Communication was via computer, and teams of students performed duties such as medical monitoring, communication, probe launching, and environment control. We were completely absorbed in solving one problem after another, and depended on each other for solutions. In a math and science enrichment program that I manage for secondary students on Saturday mornings, the place for instruction is where science happens: a pharmaceutical laboratory set up with robotics, or a geological research facility actively recording seismographic readings. We may not be able to create such simulations in our classrooms, but we do have a growing number of props to help us.

SUGGESTION FOR STANDARDS AND ENABLING ACTIVITIES

Enabling standards for learning environments should provide space for face-to-face interaction between students working in small groups, and space for activities that support and nurture variations in intelligence and student goals. Enabling activities should, where possible and indicated, move outside the classroom into more realistic spaces.

The Props of Materials and Technology

Within the classroom space setting are the many props of materials and technology that create new perceptions, lead to dissatisfaction with prior concepts, and develop plausibility and comfort with new or adapted ones. They are a vital component of enabling standards, but need to be chosen carefully. Commercial interests promote a variety of materials that easily appeal to overburdened and anxious teachers who do not have the time to create their own. Critical questions to be asked before deciding on materials include: What evidence is there that these materials will provide enabling activities that can help students reach the chosen content and performance standards? Do we know how to use them? Can they be easily replaced with more cost-effective, more culturally relevant, or more interest-stimulating substitutes?

My own program evaluation research as an educator in schools and universities as well as that of many others demonstrate the value of using concrete materials that increase perception and nurture varied intelligences, but too often the props are seen as the entire solution. For example, the omnipresent elementary science kits with hands-on materials for student exploration have intrinsic value in that they satisfy children's goals to use all their senses, and the resulting new perceptions can lead to new constructions. But to ensure the development of complex new concepts in the consensual domain—the set of universal or commonly held beliefs that constitute the content standards—the teacher-mediator still needs to set the stage for the stretch across the zone of potential construction with appropriate dialogue. This may be difficult for many elementary teachers, who are themselves uncomfortable with science concepts. Even high school science teachers sometimes neglect to make the necessary connections between the content they wish their students to learn and the cookbook labs they schedule because they are convenient and familiar.

The many new manipulatives for mathematics instruction are wonderful—I cannot envision working without them. The manipulatives are motivating and necessary because they respond to the often neglected kinesthetic intelligence, create new kinesthetic and spatial perceptions, simulate realistic problems, facilitate reasoning, and promote the construction of conceptual knowledge. But they, too, are analogies for the real thing, and are only as good as the meaningfulness of the problems they are meant to solve and the reasoning that goes into their solutions. The teacher still has to do some instructional mapping for students as they use the material to stretch students to a new concept and generalization that then works in new situations without the presence of manipulatives. I have discovered, moreover, that some children quickly reason abstractly and become annoyed with manipulatives; others, and some adults, need them longer.

Although modern textbooks are designed for eye appeal and rarely do a good job of unaided concept development, they do respond to the needs of those with linguistic and spatial intelligence, and they can be useful as one source of new perceptions. Single-topic trade books with good narrative form and other types of children's literature may be better choices that can engage students and allow them to independently construct new knowledge in their interaction with what is, after all, a social artifact. Written texts nurture and are needed for the development of linguistic intelligence. They are not an adequate or complete substitute for the teacher's dialogue, peer interactions, or other kinds of more realistic experiences, however (see Chapter 2, "Are New Standards Necessary?"). Enabling activities that combine the reading of text and writing are more effective. Mediation of the reading of texts and other literary artifacts by teachers using dialogue constructions are a necessary adjunct for most students. Particular constructions such as those used in reciprocal teaching have proven effective.

Interactive technology offers much promise. The substantive research evidence that would prove the effectiveness of technology applications to the instructional process is not yet available. Most of what we have are descriptions of students and programs in action. But when these observations are related to what we already know about what works, it is easy to predict the outcomes. Interactive technology combines goal-satisfying student control with stimulation of spatial, linguistic, and kinesthetic intelligence. It provides the immediate feedback that verifies efficacy and helps create disequilibrium if the new perceptions do not agree with prior knowledge. By offering choices at varying levels, it allows for developmental differences.

I watch my grandson, Edward, with the CD-ROM *Gizmos and Gadgets*. Without any formal reading instruction, he is reading the necessary instructions and choices in a program meant for slightly older children. When the problem is not easily surmounted, he is momentarily frustrated, discovers a way out, and tries something else. But he is also persistent with follow-up attempts to correct the same stumble. There is no one to deride his mistakes, and instant gratification for his successes. He punctuates and communicates them with a resounding "Yessss!" He prefers to have me or a peer at his side as he works, and calls for my help sometimes, but readily accepts the challenge to discover how to do it himself.

Short of worldwide travel, what better way is there to learn about our vast world culture than to correspond over the Internet with students in other countries or to access, at will, video clips that depict the places they live in? I watch 3rd and 4th graders use the PowerPoint presentation to prepare a social studies report for the class. They have researched the Internet, used an on-line encyclopedia, pulled in some video clips and their own photographs, and entered their original coordinating dialogue. The challenge for us now is to ensure equity for all students by making the enabling standards of technology a requisite adjunct to the content and performance standards, and we need to learn how to work these standards into our overall plans for constructing the classroom environment.

Technology will help us meet the challenge of new content standards and help us prepare our students for life in a technologically rich world. It must be considered as a high-priority enabling standard, but not the only one. Not all the new software is good, and we need to avoid over-dependence on it. It is all too new for us to reach any firm conclusions, but I predict that technology will never completely eliminate the need for teacher mediation of the learning process, replace the mind-stimulating experience of face-to-face peer interaction, or be a substitute for counting individual pieces of candy to achieve the concept of one-to-one correspondence.

In summary, the props of the educational theater must place the teacher and the student in the center of the enactment. The materials should not be in control; as Ball and Cohen (1996) suggest, the traditional boundaries between teachers' teaching and the material's presentation of content may need to be redrawn. One of the most powerful uses of props in theater (with devastating effect) has been the use of the cigarette. Those of us old enough to remember the scene in *Now Voyager* in which Bette Davis and Paul Henried share cigarettes will also recall, however, that it was the involvement of the performers and the power of the script that made the props work.

SUGGESTION FOR STANDARDS AND ENABLING ACTIVITIES

Enabling standards should include opportunities for teachers to learn how to choose and use educational materials (texts, packaged curriculum guides, manipulatives, and technology). Materials need to be provided and carefully articulated with the content and performance standards, as well as with varying student interests and abilities. The presence of educational technology may be a critical enabling standard. However, the enactment of curriculum by teachers and students, not the materials, should be at the center.

The Actors

The Performers and Their Director

Continuing the metaphor of classroom environment as theater, I now draw attention to the actors. In addition to the aspects of classroom management that were described above as components of the setting, it is the responsibility of the teacher-director to manage and control the actors so that they are engaged and attentive to the tasks prescribed. One key to success may be the effective management of student goals. Human goals control learning. They can promote it, but they can also undermine it. In addition to considering the prior knowledge of the learner, and reflecting on previous educational experience with a selected activity, teacher-directors must pay attention to student goals as they set up the zone of potential construction. For example, there is, undoubtedly, a strong human need to control the environment. If it appears to the individual that new knowledge is required for this control, then the learner will probably "go for it." If learning what others have prescribed appears to the individual to have nothing to do with personally desired control of the environment, or more significantly the prescription for learning interferes with other personal goals, there is instead resistance.

A 3rd grader who has not met with much success in learning mathematics experiences little sense of power or efficacy when that subject is being taught, and may make an effort at that time to satisfy more personal goals. The time may be used to gain the attention and approbation of peers with a joke, or to play with a more interesting new toy; the student satisfies a competing social goal and is disengaged. Other goals such as social compliance can, for a while, overcome this distraction; goal revision via experiences of success, planned and strengthened by effective teaching, will work the best over time.

A hungry elementary child may be dealing with physical urges that wipe out other stimuli. An emotionally insecure middle school preadolescent or a high school student concerned with personal safety may find it difficult to put aside the retrieval of conflicting memories and ideas. In each case, the zone of construction of new knowledge is too wide or nonexistent. Prior relevant knowledge is not retrieved, and new perceptions are unprocessed.

Preemptive Goal Management

The techniques that teachers may employ in the task of nurturing goals that positively mediate learning can be divided into preemptive and contingent-corrective categories. Preemptive goal management can be embedded in the enabling activities, but contingent-corrective management of students' goals usually boils down to the behavioral punishment and reward procedures of traditional classroom discipline. Both require an understanding of human goals.

New knowledge gained from recent research has added to extensive prior findings that explain how goals control the learning process, but also result in some theory revision. Early emphasis in the investigation of the relationship between motivation and achievement focused on the influences of human needs such as the need for power, the need for achievement, and the need for affiliation (Murray, 1938, cited in Urdan & Maehr,

1995). Later research examined the differential achievement of students motivated either by task (mastery) goals, which value the outcome of learning for its intrinsic value of knowing, or by performance (ability) goals, which, more egotistically, value the social prestige that higher grades or other evidences bring from comparisons with others. In these studies, task goals were associated with more effective performance, greater retention, and more in-depth knowledge (Dweck & Leggett, 1988; Pintrich et al., 1993). The two kinds of goals appeared at first to be dichotomous and mutually exclusive—students motivated by either one or the other.

Recent evidence has shown the influence of goals to be much more complicated. A variety of social goals has the potential for both positive and negative effects on achievement depending on the cultural norms and the particular context (Wentzel, 1989, 1993). For example, in cultures where achievement is valued as a contribution to the group rather than as an accomplishment for the individual, the more social performance goals have the same effect on learning as task-mastery goals. Goals based on compliance with parents and teachers may be more effective in societies or ethnic groups where the sense of self is derived from affiliation with parents. A strong task-mastery goal orientation may even be dysfunctional in a society where group rather than individual efforts are rewarded.

Even within heterogeneous populations, the desire by an individual for affiliation with a high-performing peer group can result in greater achievement. In contrast, the need for acceptance by a low-performing peer group can have the opposite effect. In some situations, it may be beneficial to have a combination of task-mastery and ability-performance goals. Cooperative learning environments that provide structures for individual accountability and group interdependence are examples of multiple goals acting in tandem.

A substantial body of research has investigated the relationship between achievement and self-concept (Anderman & Maehr, 1994). A strong self-concept generally has been associated with better performance. Recently, self-concept has been recognized as a complex construct that can be subdivided into subcategories such as self-worth, self-esteem, or sense of self in relation to others (how do I compare), and self-efficacy or the "beliefs in one' s capabilities to organize and execute the courses of action required to manage prospective situations" (Bandura, in press, cited in Pajares, 1996, p. 2). Feelings of self-efficacy that are related to a specific task (I can learn to skate well) seem to have a greater effect on ultimate performance than more general feelings of positive self-esteem (I am a capable person).

Many researchers seek to demonstrate that variations in general self-esteem explain the differences between performances, but find ambivalent evidence that they do. Those who hypothesized that differences between various ethnic groups can be attributed to differences in self-esteem have in recent studies found these differences to be changing over time and less significant or ambivalent predictors of varying performance then previously believed (see Cooper & Dorr, 1995; Graham, 1995).

Teachers should, however, be interested in the considerable effects of self-efficacy on the construction of knowledge. Self-efficacy is much more specific in that it relates to a specific task rather than an overall feeling about one's ability. That specificity makes it a stronger predictor of ultimate performance (Pajares, 1996).

The motto "believe you can achieve" is posted all over a school I visit frequently, and I am sure that it has some positive self-esteem effect, but it is Melinda O'Neill, a teacher who provides carefully chosen, step-by-step, developmentally appropriate, transitional experiences and supportive dialogue, who reinforces the students' confidence to achieve a particular task and ensures the best performance. She begins her buildup of self-effacacy by giving students choices for activities within their cooperative groups; when they successfully complete the easier ones, she slowly cajoles them with cautious encouragement to try harder ones. Enabling standards should include a range of activities that reinforce competence and challenge students further. They may also have to include opportunities for teachers to learn how to assess, manage, and change student goals preemptively just as they have done correctively in the past.

SUGGESTION FOR ENABLING STANDARDS AND ACTIVITIES

Content standards should include step-by-step progressions that allow students to gain self-efficacy in particular tasks. Matching performance standards should allow for multiple assessment forms that will not undermine self-efficacy. Task mastery goals are more effective than performance goals and have longevity. Although we want students to attempt new tasks because they feel good about achieving the tasks—not because they want to be better than their peers—cultural and microsocial variations in the weight of task-mastery and performance goals and in social compliance goals should be considered. Combinations of these goals may be a viable alternative. Cooperative learning activities can provide this kind of preemptive goal management.

Contingent-Corrective Goal Management

Gold stars have been around for a long time. They have been somewhat replaced by happy face stickers and other tokens. My grandson, Edward, gets them on his nursery school papers all the time. He has never pointed them out to me. Instead he proudly displays the new letter he has written all by himself on the back of the ditto sheet that requires him to trace the letter. Although teachers have consistently used contingent extrinsic rewards such as gold stars with apparent effect as a means of controlling student goals, there is evidence that, when expected, these rewards may not be the most effective form of goal management in that they undermine the pursuit of intrinsic rewards and consequent self-motivation for further engagement in similar tasks (Kohn, 1993, 1996; Lepper, Keavney, & Drake, 1996; Ryan & Deci, 1996).

In some cases where the culture or the home environment is itself highly structured with contingent rewards, the child's expectations of such rewards may be so great that they are the teacher's only recourse, but other tactics should be tried. Unexpected contingent rewards do not seem to affect intrinsic motivation. Some teachers detach rewards from specific tasks, and instead surprise students with tokens from time to time. I watched some 3rd graders quickly open their desks after lunch to see if there was a surprise for someone from their teacher. These tokens seem to be a way of establishing an affiliation with the teacher, who rewards them in a general way rather than for a specific task. Verbal reinforcement can also be used profitably if it addresses the content more specifically than if it is a general expression of praise. For example, the teacher comment, "Using the Internet to get some information really helped your report" may be more supportive of intrinsic motivation than "That was an excellent report."

It is beyond the scope of this chapter and book to discuss the various methods of correction used to control student goals, but these methods have been a standard response to the constant struggle for power that exists in any classroom. Teachers' goals for controlling the learning process and their imperative to construct new knowledge conflict with student needs for autonomy and the satisfaction of other social goals that may not be learning directed. Time for teacher-designed learning tasks will be curtailed by student disengagement, either in pursuit of these other goals or by the other distractions of today's schools. Even in my graduate classes and in the halls of Congress, an order to "cease and desist" activity that takes time from the task intended is sometimes needed. It works if it is used infrequently—like an extrinsic reward diminishing in its effectiveness with every use. Enabling standards that are preemptive goal managers, that establish time-saving routines, and that protect the space of the learning environment from unnecessary and extraneous interference are more effective. Enabling activities that grab the student's attention with interest and nurture the satisfaction of intrinsic goals offer the greatest promise.

SUGGESTION FOR STANDARDS AND ENABLING ACTIVITIES

Corrective goal management works best if it is limited to specific verbal reinforcement of the content task or surprise rewards that promote a general sense of affiliation and recognition. General verbal reinforcements and contingent rewards such as gold stars have only a transitory effect. They may, however, be necessary and useful at some times with some students and in some classrooms. Other forms of correction may also be necessary to gain attention, but they lose effectiveness with increased use. Enabling standards and activities should provide for the more effective correctives so that attention and momentum are ensured.

The Script

The Overall Plot

The third pivot in the metaphor of constructing learning environments as theater is the script: the overall plot and the dialogue. These are at the heart of the enabling standards that match and accomplish content and performance standards. They are often not adequately planned for. I am not recommending that teachers walk into every class with prescribed inflexible scripts (a direct instruction method that was suggested at one time), but there are patterns that work that should become part of every teacher's repertoire. For overall plot, there are proven effective models such as inquiry, jurisprudential inquiry, role playing, reciprocal teaching, synectics, concept attainment, and induction (see Joyce & Weil, 1996, for descriptions of these models). They can be copied as a whole or combined in different ways to meet varying needs. What they have in common is a problem-solving organization that builds on intrinsically motivating goals and a structure that maps new perceptions and challenges students to make new complex connections instead of simply recalling what they hear or read. These connections enable students to construct new or adapted knowledge. When combined with cooperative learning, these models can promote the intersubjective construction of new knowledge, knowledge that is new to all the interacting actors, students, and teachers (Lerman, 1996).

What I miss most about teaching only science classes is the ease with which I could motivate my students to pursue the solution to a problem and the thrill of discovering something new along with them. I still try to use the presentation of anomalous data or a discrepant event whenever I can. Like scientists, students (and most adults in everyday situations) are intrinsically motivated by the need to solve a problem or explain something that has unexpectedly happened or that does not agree with previous perceptions. Problem solving can be an effective framework for the overall script plot in any domain. The problem can be posed by the teacher or by students in response to an experience planned by a teacher, or it can arise spontaneously from student needs and experiences.

Planning for a field day can evolve into: How can we predict the weather for our field day? How should we lay out the baseball diamond so that the sun is not in anyone's eyes when we play? How can we discover what soft drink most kids prefer? How can we elect judges for the contests who are representative of the whole school? What should we say in our invitations to parents and the community and how can we advertise it best? What artifacts should we choose in the time capsule we bury?

In the Saturday morning enrichment program that is part of the Mc-Extend teacher network, each curriculum unit is organized around a specific relevant problem, such as, "What are the chances for an earthquake in our county?" Students collect data from observations in the field and from current and historical seismographic reports, and then they interpret the data and make projections. This kind of problem solving is different from the historical application of word problems at the back of a chapter in math or physics books. Those follow teacher-demonstrated rules, procedures, and previously practiced algorithms. Instead, teachers in problem-centered math programs do not "expect all children to use a particular algorithm" and they allow their students to "spend a great deal of time working out their own procedures for solving . . . problems and sharing and discussing alternate strategies with their classmates" (Carpenter et. al., 1994, p. 4). Ultimately, after making the necessary connections between the problems and the physical representations that can be used to solve them, students design their own algorithms.

A problem-solving structure works in other subject areas as well. Recent studies of the reading and writing connection illustrate that the need to synthesize and analyze information from texts when it is required for writing analytic essays enhances the comprehension of the reading material. Simple summaries that do not require synthesis are less effective

(Greene & Ackerman, 1995). Other problem-solving connections to the reading of text material are effective. When learning about the models of teaching described above, my students must cooperatively demonstrate one of the models. Their absorption and long-term retention of the models they demonstrate is evidenced by its appearance and clarity in later portfolios and in their student teaching. They have some difficulty with other models that they just read about and see demonstrated, but a graphic organizer that requires them to analyze the similarities and differences in two models, with justification, has proven very helpful. It is a "double bubble," but other forms of concept mapping are also useful. This brings us to the dialogue.

The Dialogue

The settings and props may frame the script, and patterns such as those of the models mentioned above may develop the themes of the plot, but the enacted curriculum as the performers experience it is essentially improvisational. Classroom ethnographers have documented what we educators always knew: that "students' goals and their understanding of the objectives of the task can transform the task to the point that it is no longer the same as what was intended by the teacher." In addition, the teacher "can wittingly or (unwittingly) change the nature of tasks by stressing less or more challenging aspects of the task or by altering the resources" (Stein, Grover, & Henningsen, 1996, p. 460).

If the teacher has clear outcomes in mind, there is less chance of loss of learning opportunity as control shifts to the student performers. Instead, the improvisations can be made to work as effectively as any planned script. In reciprocal teaching, for example, metacognitive strategies for attacking the text such as question generation, summarization, predictions, and clarification are first purposely modeled, but then students are encouraged to challenge each other's interpretations with self-constructed elaborations, reflections, and questions. This method has been demonstrated to increase comprehension. You have to listen to respond.

The teacher-director does not abdicate in the discourse. This is the opportunity for scaffolding the algorithmic level of brain processing addressed in Chapter 3, "What We Now Know About How Learning Happens." This is where attention is captured to heighten new perceptions; cues are offered to help retrieve prior knowledge, including previous generalizations; questions are asked to help make connections and new generalizations; and learning-supporting goals are managed to mitigate the construction. This is where we get to higher-order thinking.

Clarity for the student in the task itself and in the new constructions of knowledge are the teacher's constant responsibility. Actions reflect what is happening at the moment and previous teaching experience. Many of the actions are assessments, which I discuss in detail in Chapter 6, "How Are We Doing? Measuring Success." The director interprets and responds to the assessments and aims for the further stretch across the zone of construction. In reciprocal teaching and in other forms of scaffolding or instructional mapping, the tasks and dialogue are set up by the teacher, and as the tasks progress, they are fermented[2] by further discourse tosses (questions, paraphrases, etc.) from the teacher (see Rosenshine & Meister, 1994; Cohen, 1994).

The script can include the materials and proven techniques such as advance and graphic organizers. The dialogue can consist of directions, questions, and requests for questions. There may also be nonverbal cues such as a puzzled look, pointing to another child to ask for a response or reaction, a smile, a thumbs up, or hand motions asking for additions.

The research on instructional mapping in mathematics education is especially strong. Educators are recording the thinking processes of students as they confront problems and use materials to try to solve problems, but they are also examining the effects of various forms of questions and dialogues. Here are some of the direction and question patterns I encourage future math teachers to use:

- How did you get your answer?
- Show us how you used your materials to get your answer.
- Is there another way to get that answer?
- Does anyone have another answer?
- Can you prove your answer?
- Can you think of another problem that can be solved in the same way?
- Try this problem with smaller quantities.
- Act out this problem, or make a picture of it.
- Share your reasoning with your partner.
- Write about what you just learned so that someone else can learn from it.

A quote from Vygotsky (1962, p. 104, cited by Rosenshine & Meister, 1994, p. 484) also seems appropriate here:

In the child's development imitation and instruction play a major role. . . . Therefore, the only good kind of instruction is that which marches ahead of development and leads it; it must be aimed not so much at the ripe, but at the ripening functions.

This is not far from the high expectations our new standards are calling for. The only thing keeping us from a sell-out performance is the right setting, motivated performers, a good script, and the best director we can find. Additional suggestions for enabling standards and activities appear below and criteria for predicting their overall success are offered in Table 5.1.

SUGGESTION FOR STANDARDS AND ENABLING ACTIVITIES

Enabling standards should provide for overall patterns or models of teaching that furnish a framework for metacognitive strategy development, task-mastery goals, self-constructed knowledge, and maximum active interaction. Problem-solving frameworks, inquiry designs, and reciprocal teaching and concept attainment forms, especially effective in combination with cooperative learning, are examples. Enabling activities within these models should allow for some student task control, question generation, syntheses, and reflective evaluations. Teachers should direct the enabling activities with supportive dialogue, instructional mapping, or scaffolding—constantly stretching students toward levels higher than those already attained.

Notes

1. There are some exceptions. By special legislative action, for example, the state of New York prescribes the teaching of some specific curriculum fragments such as Arbor Day, the humane treatment of animals, drug education, and the potato famine in Ireland.

2. *Fermenting* is a term used in cooperative learning. It implies that the teacher or the group must make the discourse go beyond simple recall into higher-order thinking skills such as analysis, synthesis, and evaluation.

TABLE 5.1   Criteria for Assessing Enabling Standards and Activities

(Teachers should add their own criteria to this list)

Enabling standards and activities address the learning environment, the in-and-out of school experiences, and the materials and personnel required.

The enabling standards and activities: (Check all that apply and comply)

_____ Articulate with content and performance standards (are designed to help students meet them).

_____ Provide for the necessary allocations of space and time.

_____ Provide the teacher with necessary skills and support.

_____ Group students heterogeneously in small within-class groups that are inter-dependent.

_____ Provide opportunities for students to develop self-efficacy in terms of specific tasks.

_____ Reflect multicultural differences and changes in student needs for affiliation, their motivations to achieve, and their interests.

_____ Provide for greater preemptive goal management and less contingent rewards and corrective discipline.

_____ Provide for carefully selected proven effective curriculum materials that reflect all the above.

_____ Have structures that are built around finding solutions to student-relevant problems, and use constructive models such as inquiry, concept attain-ment, role-playing, and induction.

_____ Are flexible or varied enough to meet the needs of all student learning styles.

_____ Have teacher-directed dialogues that encourage students to reflect, syn-thesize, and evaluate new perceptions and ideas and respond with their own self-generated questions.

_____ Are designed to stretch the student from present levels of knowledge to new generalizations at higher levels constantly.

6

How Are We Doing?

Measuring Success

M y friend Bonnie, who is a drama coach, questioned my use of the theater as a metaphor for creating the classroom environment. Her point, which was well taken, was that the performers in a drama put on masks, and classrooms should be places where students are themselves. Upon reflection, I am not so sure that this is what really exists. Even as they are evaluating themselves, much of what students and their teachers do in schools is for the purpose of demonstrating to others. On the classroom stage, teacher- and student-performers constantly demonstrate what they know to each other and productively use the demonstrations to help direct and motivate further actions. Schools also have off-stage and demanding audiences, parents and the public at large, for whom they must demonstrate that the time and resources spent on education are effective. Like good theater, a well-communicated demonstration for others, whether it is within the action on stage or directed toward the audience, sometimes involves putting on a special face or mask.

When demonstrations go beyond the purpose of communicating with others and are measured and compared to a standard, they become quality or quantity indicators of what the performer knows, has accomplished, or can do. Because they have different standards or criteria, theater critics and teachers often disagree on the same performance. Educators today even disagree about the meaning of the term *standard*. Wiggins (1995) defines standard in the singular as "an exemplary performance serving as a benchmark," in the plural as "specific and guiding pictures," and when modified to "high standards" as "a set of mature, coherent, and consistently applied values" (p. 129). In its current applications, the term *standard* is ambivalently ascribed either to descriptions of desired ends for students that have a clearly discriminated "level of the bar" or model of exemplary performance, or to descriptions that are more general principles of knowledge or values to be attained. The widely adopted standards of the National Council of Teachers of Mathematics (1989) represent the latter type and do not have levels described. Recently issued statements of standards developed by states usually begin with more general principles or values, but then attempt to attach them to a specific desired level of performance.

In previous chapters, I have distinguished between statements of standards, designating the standards that describe the knowledge or skill to be attained without reference to a level for the purpose of measurement as content standards, and statements that have inherent statements of levels as performance standards. This chapter adds greater detail to the meaning and role of content and performance standards in framing instruction, the measures within them, and the instruments used to take these measures.

Standards and Their Measures

Standards may be defined, interpreted, applied, and measured in many different but often overlapping ways. To begin with, it is important to remember that there is a strong human imperative to judge oneself. Standards may be the performer's own, and the measure may be one of self-evaluation. An infant takes great pleasure in his first successful attempt to reach for something or to stand, not because he measures himself against an external standard, but because he has a strong human need to have power over the environment in which he finds himself. Our ability to control the environment is an internal standard that is with us always. Although we may make revisions and modifications in response to other goals, we measure ourselves against this standard until we die.

The common connotation for performance standards is that they are externally imposed measures. This may be the case if we do not create environments in which students are motivated to set their own performance standards and take their own measures—or at least measure themselves against a standard that they understand and accept. Nevertheless, we live in a social world and respect externally imposed standards because they represent the consensual domain of knowledge and skills. The revisions we make in our own standards are most often based on what we observe others able to do and on the judgments of others. Schools and their students owe their audiences clearly communicated evidence that

TABLE 6.1 Self-Assessment

Self-Evaluation of Portfolio Element

Why did you select this portfolio element?

What did you like the most about doing this portfolio element?

What did you like the least about doing this portfolio element?

What is good about the work that you have done for this portfolio element?

What could be improved in the work that you have done for this portfolio element?

What are the 10 most important things that you learned about biology from doing this portfolio element?

Share your work with two of your classmates. What did they like about your portfolio element?

Share your work with two of your classmates. What suggestions did they have for improving your portfolio element?

What advice should your teacher give to future students who might select a portfolio element similar to this one?

SOURCE: University of the State of New York, 1997.

they are meeting expectations. It is our own constant measure of how we ourselves are progressing, however, that directs us and drives us over a lifetime to ever higher levels of achievement.

When Gary Kasparov walked away from his final defeat in his well-publicized chess tournament with IBM's Big Blue computer, he did so in a huff. It was a simple win-or-lose measure that disappointed him for the moment, but did not discourage him from quickly issuing a new challenge. He admitted that he had underestimated the abilities of his opponent, but a more carefully prepared for rematch would prove his human invincibility. Kasparov then busily engaged himself in studying his own errors and the skills of his computer opponent in anticipation of another challenge. Unfortunately, educators' measures of students' progress are not always so clear cut, and, more often than not, they do not challenge us or our students to try harder or motivate us to find out exactly why we were unsuccessful. Although we constantly assess students in informal ways as we teach them, we rarely openly attribute the student's lack of success to our own performance. How often have you heard a teacher say, "I am sorry that you didn't understand, perhaps I didn't do a good job of explaining what was needed." Nor do we often enough engage and encourage students to evaluate themselves methodically and consciously. Modeling of self-assessment by teachers and more structured opportunities for self-evaluation by students such as the one in Table 6.1 might be helpful.

The standards or levels of the bar against which we most frequently measure ourselves in schools are socially determined. And though we usually accept the results as personal, these measured demonstrations are often designed for the benefit of another audience and for different purposes. It is important to understand the differences in the purpose of measured demonstrations, or *assessments,* as they are commonly referred to when they are more systematically applied (Herman, Aschbacher, & Winters, 1992), because even though they may overlap, different purposes require different measures.

The Purposes of Measures or Assessments

Students' various on- and off-stage audiences—themselves, their peers, their teachers, their parents (at times in the role of teacher), and the public at large—represent different purposes for assessment. As they interact with the environment, students need to measure themselves in terms of personal goals such as the ability to control that environment. The interactive responses they get from their peers and the informal and formal assessments by their teachers are among the measures they use. And depending on the strength of affiliate goals such as self-efficacy, social compliance, and task or performance motivation (see Chapter 5, "Constructing Creative Classrooms"), these assessments may or may not positively affect the learning process. The assessments may also frame new goals or modify existing ones.

Teachers in the students' on-stage audience take constant informal measures within activities and classroom discourse, reflect on these measures, and then adjust the discourse or the learning environment in response. This most important purpose for measurement has also been the most unrecognized. The standards against which teachers make informal classroom assessments are not usually stated in written form: They are more often subliminal and intuitive, based on teachers' knowledge, their prior experience with children, and their own learning experiences. The informal assessments may be systematized, however, in oral questioning patterns and in the materials within the enabling activities. Teachers may at times also assess themselves in relation to their informal assessments of students, but their self- and student measures usually place greater weight on more formal assessments such as oral and written tests, probably because these can also have the purpose of informing a different audience: school administrators, parents, and the public at large.

Parents and the public have an important investment in the education of students. They are a critical and demanding audience. Formal assessments such as traditional standardized tests are meaningful to this audience because they believe that the tests are controlled, reliable, and valid. Although only broadly assessing the child's individual progress and rarely diagnosing specific needs, these assessments provide comparison to a norm and allow parents to position their children and their schools in relation to others. Educated parents recognize the highly competitive culture in which we live, and worry about their offspring's chances for success. Better assessments of individual progress matched to clarified performance standards might be able to sway parents from preoccupation with these incompletely revealing measures. They may also have greater meaning for the many uninformed parents who do not understand standardized and normed[1] tests and may consider them unfair and biased for children whose cultures may be different from the norming sample.

On a broader scale, the public audience demands accountability for the dollars spent on education, and attributes socioeconomic problems to school failure. The purpose of assessment in this case is to evaluate the system rather than the individual child. Although system measures require the levels of objectivity, validity, and reliability that we have endowed on our traditional standardized tests, we may not need to use them in such a pervasive and controlling way. They also need careful interpretations.

Much of the recent effort on the part of political entities to instill higher standards and uniformity has been based on unfavorable comparisons of the children of this country with the performance of children from other nations on international tests. Although the recently published results of the Third International Math and Science Study (TIMSS) showed some improvement over previous studies (more so in science than in math), the results are still disappointing (Schmidt et al, 1996). Concerns about our students' performance continue. In a press release, Secretary of Education Richard Riley explained that even though our own assessments, the National Assessments of Educational Progress (NAEP), show improvement in math since the early 1980s, because students in other nations are also moving up, the improvement is not good enough (www.ed.gov/pressreleases/11-96/timss.html).

Some educators believe that we have exaggerated the deficiencies and perhaps incorrectly attributed them to poor performance on the part of schools and educators (Bracey, 1997). They suggest that we have neglected to examine other contributing factors such as the wide disparities in our own population, and failed to consider the perhaps unfavorable emphasis on tests and resulting pressures on students in other countries. This may be true if one considers the *jukus*[2] of Japan, but even our neighbor Canada gets better results.

The TIMSS elucidated some possible causes such as unfocused curriculum and materials and less time for teachers to prepare. It also found that the typical goal of U.S. mathematics teachers is to teach students how to do something, whereas the goal of Japanese teachers is to help students understand mathematical concepts (Stedman, 1997). These diagnosed differences need to be addressed, but I agree with Baker (1997), who believes that fixating on national achievement as "some sort of educational Olympiad" is problematic. He admits that ranking may be useful in a limited way, but suggests that "international studies are most useful . . . when they are used to shed light on why a country produces a particular pattern of achievement" (p. 16). Light and clarity help us communicate with our public audience.

Although Kasparov's actions in achieving his goal were extremely complex, the goal itself was clear, and the win-or-lose measure was an objective and simple dichotomy. Clarity in the standards we use in schools as informal and formal benchmarks or levels of the bar are rarely so objective or simple. The results of formal assessments such as standardized tests are often openly reported, but the content standards on which they are based are unclear. Informal standards are rarely stated. If standards are to serve as a guide for instruction and for self-measures, greater clarity is necessary. For the measurements we make for other audiences, greater clarity is a sine qua non.

The Consequences of Assessments

Greater clarity is particularly critical when assessments are designed for a public audience and are "high-stakes" measures. Any evaluation of performance that has long-term and psychological consequences, such as class placement or college acceptance, can be a high-stakes measure. Two recent incidents illuminate the need for this clarity. In Chicago, a city that had been criticized for its failures to educate its students, 8th and 9th graders were not allowed to graduate until they passed tests that measured their achievement of higher standards. They would have to go to summer school and retake the tests. In New York City, hundreds of community college students were told 2 weeks before graduation that they would not receive diplomas because they had not passed an English proficiency test that was mandated just before their graduation was scheduled.

These highly publicized incidents were met with mixed reactions. Students and their friends and relatives were emotionally traumatized. Their personal expectations and feelings of self-efficacy were greatly affected. In contrast, there was much support from the unaffected public that applauded the implementation of "higher standards." Teachers were pleased that they now could use the real threat of nonpromotion or nongraduation to get students to work harder.

The public distress caused by these incidents could have been avoided if there had been greater clarity in the standards from the beginning. Standards need to be transparent, in that they are free of deceit. After the fact impositions of standards with high-stakes consequences are unfair and may in the long run be unproductive. In New York, where new assessments are being planned to be phased in over a 5-year period, the changes have been preceded by public hearings with Richard Mills, the state commissioner of education. The hearings have been helpful preparation for these changes. They have provided useful information to the public officials, who discovered unpredicted anxiety among the public and educators. Those who make decisions about high-stakes measures can benefit from listening to the voices of those affected (Solomon, 1995).

High-stakes measures are not always so public. The measures that determine placement in gifted programs, special education, or acceptance to college are usually private and sometimes secretive. A high-stakes measure for students may not be one for teachers, and the opposite may also be true. Standardized tests may be of little consequence for students but of great concern for teachers, and they have good reason for this. Administrators may use test results to help make tenure or class assignment decisions. Knowledgeable parents tend to evaluate the quality of their children's schools and teachers on the basis of these. States issue public "report cards" that advertise results in an open and dramatic way. In several states, low-performing schools or districts are taken over by the state education departments.

High-stakes measures may have a negative and limiting influence on curriculum. A study of the time spent by elementary teachers in preparing their students for standardized tests (Madaus et al., 1992) reveals that teachers in minority schools spend considerably more time at this than teachers in nonminority schools. Teachers at different levels are also affected differently. Elementary teachers are more likely than high school teachers to be concerned about their students' performance on standardized tests. But the recent emphasis on high standards has made all teachers sensitive to the possible consequences of high-stakes measures. The team of teachers engaged in writing a new science curriculum may have just such a test on their minds.

Where Should Meg, April, and Brad Begin?

We left the science curriculum writing team in Chapter 5, "Constructing Creative Classrooms," as they began their task. Not too far into the task, Brad brought up a real concern. "Well, these content and performance standards we are writing are fine for your kids, but what about my ESL students? They are having a hard enough time with the state test now." Meg and April were not without anxiety either. Although their students had usually done fairly well on the tests, each new administration or version brought some trepidation that perhaps they as teachers hadn't covered everything. Parents always seemed more interested in these results than in other things the kids were bringing home. And the annual press release comparing their school with others in the region was sometimes an embarrassment.

April, always the most concerned with content coverage, quickly suggested, "Let's look at all the old tests and write our standards based on these." Where high-stakes tests are mandated, it may be helpful to look carefully at previously administered samples. Teachers owe their students preparation for these, but it is a mistake to allow such measures to limit what they want to do. As the common aphorism "what gets tested gets taught" tells us, tests can drive the curriculum (Resnick & Resnick, 1989). They can also narrow it, calling attention away from what may be more important but not tested. Content and performance standards that are more broadly based, that take into consideration the individual needs, learning styles, and current culture of students, should prevent this and pave the way to useful measures.

As soon as the team chooses the content standards it wishes to achieve—from those that are mandated and those that team members themselves feel are worthy—it can immediately write end-result levels of achievement into the performance standards. These will help the team know where they want their students to go. Finding measures that will mark on-the-way progress that are useful and meaningful to the many audiences will be a greater challenge. As team members construct curriculum and implement it, they need to think about the intermediate steps that lead to the desired results, and then build matching assessments that will keep them and their students informed of progress. Informal measures and more systematic assessments can be integrated right into enabling activities.

Some teachers have developed assessment patterns that they use all the time. Journal writing is an example of this. If the journal goes beyond recording events and requires the student to reflect on what has been learned, it can be a documented self-assessment measure and work to guide further instruction. Questioning patterns that are purposely directed toward assessing results can be routinely inserted into classroom dialogues. Videotaping the students as they work in small groups allows the teacher to review dialogue at his or her leisure, or share it with students as a self-assessment experience. Combinations of self- and peer assessments such as the one in Table 6.1 can be used to stimulate reflective interaction and improve the skills of each peer involved. Computer-managed instruction will help monitor progress, and presentation software adds easily documented and shared products. Table 6.2 contains a beginning assessment template the curriculum writing team can follow. I will add to the template as we proceed.

The steps in Table 6.2 are only a beginning. Day-to-day measures may aim for the end-result level, but intermediate steps toward the ends and intermediate measures or levels of performance will have to be decided on. Many individual adjustments will be necessary.

TABLE 6.2 Getting Started on Assessment

- Decide on your content standards (what you want your students to know or be able to do). Base these on many criteria including any mandated curriculum and tests (see below and Chapter 4).

- Describe the end-result level that will tell you that your students have accomplished each content standard. This becomes your performance standard.

- Make a list of the audiences who will be interested in measures of how your students achieved the results. Be sure to include the students themselves, yourself, supervisors, parents, and other publics.

- Clarify the purposes of the measures for each audience.

- Clarify the consequences of the measures for each audience.

- Decide where you will place more formal systematic assessments and what form they will take.

- Plan to include some assessment in each enabling activity. Developing a pattern that can be repeated in each is a good way to monitor informal measures.

- Use technology to help whenever you can

Brad may allow his ESL students to demonstrate what they know in different ways than Meg and April. Meg may have to examine her hands-on activities, identify the science concepts embedded within them, and make sure these concepts are measured. April will need to reconsider her dependence on texts if the new standards require students to analyze data and solve realistic problems. New forms of assessments will be needed to match the new curriculum. If, like so many other teachers, our threesome is engaged in this task, at the end of the 20th century, a major question on their minds will probably be, How can we make our assessments authentic? Many of the things they may already have in mind are authentic, but some clarification is now needed.

Traditional Versus Alternative Assessments

This brings us to the current debate on the relative value of traditional and authentic or alternative assessments. It may be worthwhile to review some traditional measures before I discuss the alternatives. Like the many influences on curriculum, the origins of traditional tests fall on a continuum that at one end includes wide-scale distally produced tests such as the Second International Mathematics and Science Study (SIMSS) and TIMSS, national tests such as the NAEP, and the many commercially produced exams such as the College Board's SAT, the Stanford Achievement Test, and the California Achievement Tests that are widely used across the country. In the middle of this continuum are statewide assessments such as the New York State Regents Exams and the California, New Jersey, and Oregon assessments. At the other end of the continuum are the more proximal small group or individual teachers' classroom tests.

The distally produced tests have generally been limited (with some variation) to multiple choice items because these are easy to standardize, norm, and validate. Middle-range assessments that may have started out differently have tended to follow suit. For example, early regents exams required extensive essay answers. They were shifted to strictly short answer and multiple choice formats in the 1950s and 1960s. Some of the teachers' own tests tended to follow the same pattern. Commercially produced accompaniments to texts and electronic scoring facilities made this format easy to apply and score. Tests that asked only for choices and with little opportunity for student-generated answers became the conventional form.

Unfortunately, a multiple choice test is out of sync with the more constructive demands of real life. In personal living and in the workplace, picking the correct answer from four or five stated choices is a rarely used skill. For the potential employer, the ability to create answers is what is highly prized. For the teacher, multiple choice testing does not lend itself to the kind of analysis that would help guide instruction. For the student test taker, it does not provide the kind of specific feedback that might strengthen task-mastery goals.[3] Therefore, even when they have been high-stakes measures, the traditional formal measures of standardized tests have not been productively used. Teachers either discounted them as unrelated, or were so intimidated by the high-stakes consequences of these measures that they abdicated their rights to make better decisions about what their students needed and just "taught to the test." In both cases, they saw the tests as a separate entity: separate from what they taught or separate from what they wanted to teach.

As part of the general reform movement to improve education, this kind of testing was identified by some educational leaders (e.g., Wiggins, 1989, 1996) as a source of some of our educational problems. Assessment was identified as the driving force in curriculum (what gets tested gets taught); the multiple choice tradition was lambasted as unrelated to real-life situations and demands and declared dysfunctional as an appropriate guide for instruction. *Alternative* and *authentic* are terms that have been used synonymously to describe a variety of assessments that are performance based or require a student to demonstrate or generate an answer instead of simply making a choice. As opposed to conventional multiple choice tests, performance-based assessments are envisioned to require students to "actively accomplish complex and significant tasks, while bringing to bear prior knowledge, recent learning and relevant skills to solve realistic or authentic problems" (Herman et al., 1992, p. 2). They are more subjectively scored, but also promise to be more useful instructional elements themselves and more efficient as guides for instruction.

Independent university-affiliated educational research groups such as the Center for Research on Evaluation, Standards, and Student Testing (CRESST) are leading efforts to make assessment more authentic. States have also taken some leadership in reforming assessments. Recently, in a responding shift, some New York State Regents Exams have begun to include varied performance items. Vermont has made some major shifts toward portfolio assessments, and Oregon legislated a requirement for students to demonstrate their knowledge with performances. Many more efforts are being made at the school district level (Hatenbach et al., 1997), and individual schools and teachers are producing examples such as the ones in Tables 6.6 through 6.10.

Although the major difference between alternative and conventional tests is the requirement of student-generated answers or performances rather than a choice from already prepared ones, there are some major constructive, implementation, and consequential differences as well— and these present renewed assessment challenges for educators. Table 6.3 compares some of the conventional and alternative options, and the challenges of alternative assessments are discussed below.

Challenge 1: Establishing Validity, Clarifying and Covering Constructs

One of the important criteria used by professional conventional test makers to judge the quality of assessments is the tests' validity. Establishing validity requires us to ask these questions: Does the question or the performance task measure what we want it to? Does it limit itself to measuring what we want it to (the desired concept or skill), and does it not require unaccounted for additional constructs? This second question has been particularly significant in the condemnation of conventional tests as biased. For example, a question that is set in the suburban mall experience might contain the requirement of unrelated prior knowledge constructs that may be missing from inner-city or rural students. Wide-scale alternative testing based on realistic problem solving may present a greater challenge in establishing this kind of validity. What is realistic in terms of experience for one student may not be realistic for another. We may have to come to consensus first on what is in the experience of most children or discount the particular situation and expect the student to be able to generalize from one situation to another—a worthy skill. But then we have to prepare our students for this and count the ability to generalize as well.

Before we can ask whether the assessment measures what we want it to, we must know what we want. Among the advantages of conventional testing is its ability to get at very specific concepts with relative ease. Although in their focus on the actions of the enabling activities teachers

TABLE 6.3 Comparing Conventional and Alternative Assessment Options

Option	Response Type	Objectivity of Scores; Scorer	Classification
True-false item	Responses are selected	Objectively scored: Answers are pre-determined by educators	Conventional assessment
Multiple-choice item			
Matching			
Modified Objective		Subjective scoring: may also be scored by self and/or peers	
Completion	Constructed responses: – open – free		
Short answer			
Essay			
Papers			
Lab reports	....		
Poster-board session			Alternative assessment
Portfolios			
Discussion			
Interviews			
Skills checklist			
Performance testing			
Lab/field practicals			
Projects			
Observation			

SOURCE: Reynolds, Doran, Allers, and Agruso (1996).

often forget to identify concepts, they are less likely to forget them when they are constructing tests. I have often suggested that teachers might try developing their tests before they develop their curriculum. Simultaneous construction may be the best!

When applied to current curriculum ideas and terminology, the two forms of standards—content and performance—should also be articulated and constructed in tandem. Notwithstanding this primary importance of the articulation between the content and the performance that will be used to measure it, the distinction between them is also valuable. Although it may seem redundant to some readers to make this distinction and state each separately, this procedure may help overcome past failure to clarify carefully the underlying constructs that we wish our students to attain or to match them with appropriate measures.

In the quest to develop more meaningful alternative measures of performance, there may be other unexpected outcomes. Just as assessments in the past have focused inordinately on the content constructs without attention to the applications of knowledge, we can make the corresponding mistake of placing too much emphasis on the applications and not enough on the constructs. Teachers such as Meg, who are motivated to use activities that are "doing" kinds of things, sometimes forget to map underlying constructs, even as those such as April are so focused on the content that they may forget that knowledge is as good as the ability to use it.

Therefore, although not overlooking the reality that unapplied knowledge is also unrevealed and that any measure of what is known requires a demonstration, I agree with McTighe (1996/1997, p. 7) and others that it is important to set clear *performance targets* in terms of *performances of understanding*. Although the performance may be as simple as a choice of true or false or as complex as an original musical composition, we must start with what that understanding is. Others agree. In the design of what he calls "cognitively designed assessment," Nichols (1994) describes the need for a substantive base that includes a description of the "cognitive mechanisms a performer . . . would use . . . and may include how the cognitive mechanisms develop and how more competent performers differ from less competent performers" (p. 576).

In a related perspective, Messick (1994) debates the issue of where the assessment focus should be. He distinguishes between *task-driven* performance tests, which require students to perform complex tasks and focus on the ability to perform the task itself, and performance evaluations with a *construct-driven* approach that focuses on the knowledge learned. Messick carefully examines the merits and deficiencies of each; his conclusion is that when we are assessing the concepts that the performance demonstrates (e.g., in math) rather than the performance itself (in some artistic endeavors), the construct-driven approach is best because it helps guide the selection or construction of the measurement tasks and it focuses attention on the validity of the measure.

Messick (1994) also implies that because a task-driven measure may be less focused on the underlying construct, it is less clearly subject to the criterion of validity. I agree that the validity of such assessments may be more difficult to justify, but would not want the criterion of validity to be overlooked. I also question the implication that performances themselves are not as dependent on constructs. The illustration that I often offer is that almost anyone can follow a recipe and produce a quality roux or cream sauce, but a real chef understands the concepts that explain how to balance fat, flour, and liquid, add them in the right order, and alter them to make interesting variations and additions.

I have observed that many of the newly produced alternative performance assessments do appear task-driven and neglectful of constructs. This may be because it is more difficult to break constructs down to developmental levels that can be observed in a performance than it is to break tasks down. In the analysis of different forms of rubrics in Table 6.11, developmental rubrics are judged the most difficult. Conventional testing rarely required us to do that either. It looked at constructs quantitatively rather than qualitatively. The highest score belonged to the individual who got the most items correct, rather than the individual who was functioning at the highest level. Some tests did build in different levels of difficulty so that only those who reached the highest level on each construct could achieve a very high score, but discriminating where the weaknesses were was difficult. Interestingly, new computer-based models of tests such as the Graduate Miller Analogy Test (GMAT) and the SAT do attempt to sequence questions at increasingly higher levels.[4] A student who reaches the highest level quickly may have to answer fewer questions.

The tendency to overlook constructs that are not clearly stated was demonstrated to me in two recent events. In the first case, it was the sudden realization of a graduate student art teacher as she reflected on the value of clarifying constructs. Just that day she had taken great pride in the fact that her students were able to differentiate with clarity the positive and negative space in their drawings, and that she had related the terms *positive* and *negative* to other applications of the term. But to her astonishment, she realized that although the students performed this distinction with skill, she had forgotten to help her students construct the major artistic concept that too much negative space was boring and too much positive space distracting.

The second event occurred as we reviewed an otherwise excellent curriculum unit that was disseminated within a remarkable resource guide designed to provide examples of enabling activities articulated with the content standards from the New York state curriculum (University of the State of New York, 1997). The teacher-produced unit is one example of several in the resource guide. It is an interesting and complex one based on the topic of seed dissemination that describes creatively designed performance-based enabling experiences and measures in great detail. With some additions and adjustments, the teacher used it for both 7th and 10th grades.

The unit begins with reference to the mathematics, science, and technology state standards it is designed to address. Although the standards document contains separate sections of content area standards that address broad themes and more specific constructs, there is a stronger and more specific focus on interdisciplinary general processes. The teaching unit is a clear manifestation of this emphasis. Processes covered include data gathering and interpretation, design, question development, decision making, working effectively with others, analysis of ideas, and presentation skills. The enabling activities in the unit are designed to develop many of these. Included is an opportunity for students to design their own seeds and redesign them based on collected data. There are also suggestions for students who are fast-paced learners or academically challenged, and space and time recommendations as well as safety precautions.

The assessments of performance of these processes is thorough. There are cooperative group measures as well as individual student reflections and self-evaluations with directed questions that ask the students about the purpose of the experience and their personal outcomes.

The only weak part of this otherwise remarkable unit is its minimal clarification of some basic science constructs involved in seed dissemination. The statement of content standards at the beginning addresses these only minimally as follows:

Through the observations of seed structures and methods of seed dispersal, students will construct knowledge on:

- adaptive advantages for seed dispersal to distribute seeds away from the parent plant
- adaptive advantages to intermittent dispersal of seeds as opposed to dispersing seeds all at once
- the beneficial impact of humans and animals on seed dispersal
- the close relationship between structure of seed and its function for seed dispersal. (University of the State of New York, 1997, p. 2)

The stated constructs are significant and well covered in the activities. Students should learn them with fun and permanence. The problem is that they are not connected to some important themes that would enlarge understanding. For example, the adaptive dispersal advantages of the seeds are for the purpose of minimizing competition and ensuring species survival. The beneficial effect of humans and animals on seed dispersal is an example of the interdependence of plants and animals. These important ideas could be missed in the unit. They may have arisen in the activity discussion, but they were not stated as a content or performance standard and not assessed.

The assessment of the constructs that are stated consists of four open-ended questions (University of the State of New York, 1997, p. 5) that may have a variety of correct answers, but do not demand connections to the themes mentioned above. There are also other difficulties with the questions that further illustrate the need to clarify constructs and the considerable difficulty of structuring open-ended questions. For example, although the best question, "What are some advantages of seeds getting away from the parent plant?" hints at the major construct of species survival, it can be answered simply with "To get more light and water" without ever getting to the competition or survival concept. Limiting the space for answers to two or three lines also encourages minimal responses. The second question, "Why do plants not drop all their seeds at exactly the same time?" could also get to the survival concept, but it can also be answered with a simple "They ripen at different times." The third question, "What would happen if all seeds dropped together and fell in the same spot?" could be interpreted as a repeat of the first two. The last question, "How might humans and animals help disperse seeds?" is also repetitive (and leading) if it is answered simply with "They can move them away from the parent." To get at the idea of interdependence in a less leading way, the question could be simply reworded: "What did you learn about seed dispersal that tells you something about the relationship between plants and animals?"

In a contrasting case, the value of clearly stated and understood constructs and the need for better task-driven measures as a basis for developing meaningful assessments was illustrated in the implementation of a successful long-term elementary math program change in which I was personally engaged (Solomon, 1995). To document the new curriculum, teachers produced a written K through 6 scope and sequence. It was quite different from traditional curriculums at the time, in that for each of the conventional titles or subtopics covered, the document also clarified what we called the *teleologic*, or *bottom line*, concepts (Van Lehn, 1986) that we wished our students to know. These attempted to do what Nichols (1994) suggests: predict the cognitive processes of a competent performer. The concepts and cognitive processes were grounded in ongoing research in mathematics that explored how children learn, and much of it was previously unknown by the teachers.

Each of the constructs was articulated with specific assessment criteria or performance indicators and median grade-level expectations based on our own experience as teachers. Instead of identifying a single grade level for each concept, we projected a three-stage developmental sequence range over three grades: procedural exploration, concept mastery, and procedural or algorithmic mastery. Included in the assessment criteria were many informal measures such as observations by the teacher of how the children used manipulative materials and reasoned their estimates and solutions to problems. These measures were embedded within classroom activities. There was also a formal end of the year written test, with each item matched to the specific concepts tested. Although the written document projected the three levels, it did not attach these levels or any others to specific indicators for each assessment criterion. A well-stated performance standard would have this embedded within it.

This program experience offers an additional rationale for clarifying the underlying constructs in content standards separately from the performance standards. Although the teachers engaged in implementation used a textbook at first, the clarified constructs soon became the basis for a wide range of original teacher-crafted enabling activities. If the constructs are separate and well clarified for the teacher and the student, they can not only guide the construction of planned measures but be embedded with great flexibility into the enabling activities. And these may then proffer unplanned and unpredicted measures of construct attainment.

Table 6.4 is an edited excerpt from the written document, and Table 6.5 shows a matching test item. The illustrated item was designed to match concept number 17; to address the validity criterion of not measuring unintended constructs, it should be read to children who are not yet reading at a 2nd grade level. Note how the stated constructs are measured by performances described in the criteria and embedded in the test item.

As history reveals, when assessments are too focused on constructs, they may be less meaningful and detached from the real-life applications in which the constructs will be needed; they draw attention away from these applications. As some current examples of performance measures reveal, if assessments are mainly task driven and encourage extensive preparation for a specific task, they may overlook important constructs. Potentially, they may even diminish the creativity and flexibility of the activities teachers plan, and promote just what we are trying to avoid, teaching to the test. This further narrows the curriculum. Although the negative results of teaching to the performance test can be lessened if worthy constructs are embedded in the task-driven measures, the inclination to make the measurement vehicle primary would remain. Clear presentations of equally important content and performance standards can avoid this consequence. If we value the constructs and the performances themselves, it is important to measure them well.

Challenge 2: Developing Levels of Performance, Grading

It was in the process of developing formal test items for the new math curriculum that the teachers and I began to struggle with the need for

TABLE 6.4 A Sample From a Construct Clarifying Scope and Sequence

Title	Grade Level Expectations: A. Procedural Exploration B. Concept Mastery C. Algorithmic or Procedural Mastery			Teleological Concept (content standard)	Assessment Criteria (performance standard, but with exact level markers for A, B, C left out)
	A	B	C	What students will know	How we will know what they know
17. Addition: Related facts/ to 18	K	1	2	Addition is a combining of parts to form a whole; the size of the parts and whole can be represented by symbols representing the real amounts (numbers). The symbol for the combining operation is (+)	Ability to identify parts and whole in change/result unknown combine problems Ability to construct a symbolic algorithm from the problem
18. Addition: Related facts/ to 18	1	2	3	We combine parts by adding on from one part. (Cardinal principal [knowing that the last number counted is the size of the part] must be in place.)	Correct new number by counting on. Two development levels: counting from first number in problem (COF) or largest number (COL)
30. Subtraction One digit from two digits without trading Related Facts/ to 18	1	2	3	We use subtraction to find the value of a part when we know the whole value and the value of another part. The part we don't know is the difference between the part we know and the whole. To find the difference we count up from the part or down from the whole, whichever is easier	Identification of whole, known part and difference sought from real or story problems (include comparison, change unknown, start unknown, referent unknown problems). Using real or representative materials, observed evidence of "choice" or counting up or down

TABLE 6.5 Assessment Item With Embedded Constructs

After Halloween, Ed counted his candy lollipops. He had eight (8) red ones and five (5) green ones. Make a picture that shows the whole number of lollipops. Draw a circle around the part of the lollipops that was green and another circle around the part that was red. Then fill in the missing symbols for this problem.

$$\frac{8}{()()}$$
$$()$$

indicators of the achieved performance levels for specific criteria. Although we could judge fairly well whether the student had developed the concept of part and part and whole and could generate the algorithm, it was difficult to tell whether the children could generalize without a picture or whether they had already made such a complete shift to the algorithmic procedural level that picture making was unnecessary. Facing the challenge of constructing formal items made us realize that even for informal observations, it would be helpful if there was something that would tell us at what level the student was functioning. It may be that once constructs are so clearly stated and organized in a developmental sequence, level specificity for performance assessment is not necessary, but the benefits of thinking about the levels and measuring them are worth the effort.

Because we prepared this test not only for ourselves but for a public audience with some anxieties about change, we employed a quantitative substitute for explicit levels of a construct that has been frequently used by professional test makers. Having more than one item matched to a specific concept helped us decide on classifications of mastery, partial mastery, or nonmastery for the concept. This may be useful for public audiences, but it has less value as a true diagnostic for the teacher.

The requirements of a public audience remind us to consider the connection between assessment and grading. Our embrace of conventional assessments has much to do with their commonly understood comparison grades. Most of us can interpret the apparent meaning of a 100% or A—it means we got the questions all right and did better than someone with a 90% or a B. In general, however, even though these grades may be based on an objectively scored test, they are still subjective measures against a standard. Conventional test questions are, after all, based on the expectations and skills of the test maker. They may or may not be valid measures of standards.

Nevertheless, getting a grade provides a sense of accomplishment; it may also allow us to close the door on a piece of work and go on to the next comfortably. My own students were apprehensive when, instead of giving them grades on a long-range product, I gave them ungraded ongoing extensive feedback on what was good and what still needed to be done. They wanted to know where they stood. A recent survey of high school math teachers in schools that were supposedly using new assessment forms in response to the National Council of Teachers of Mathematics (NCTM) standards revealed similar findings. Teachers wanted to grade assessments because "kids don't like to do things that aren't graded" (Senk, Beckman, & Thompson, 1997, p. 197). Although forms of assessment used included portfolios, notebooks, interviews, and oral reports, only 7% of the grade was derived from these items. The reason for skewed computation may be that graded assessments of performance items are more difficult to design and justify. Well-written rubrics are critical if we wish to add some objectivity to performance measures.

Challenge 3: Writing Rubrics

An evaluation of a student's achievement of a standard can be in terms of levels of progress toward the level of the bar or the result or in terms of the overall quality of the achievement when compared with the quality of others. In either case, descriptions of the performed behaviors that mark the intervals or comparative characteristics and provide evidence of that achievement need to be delineated. These descriptions, which are called *rubrics*, can be defined as a set of guidelines for distinguishing between performances or products of different quality. A rubric is an assessment tool that verbally describes and scales levels of student achievement on performance tasks, but it can also be associated with more conventional alphanumeric and numeric scores or grades. Rubrics should be based on the results of stated performance standards, and be composed of scaled descriptive levels of progress toward the result. They may also have levels above the stated standard result. Among other criteria for creating rubrics are

- They are understandable to students
- The scores of the scale are equidistant on a continuum (at least four scores are suggested)
- Descriptors are valid (test what you want them to) and scores are reliable (consistent)
- The highest point (level) may be above the result of the performance standard
- Scores relate to empirically validated actual levels of student performance

- The scale types include holistic (overall performance) and analytic (dimensions); the assessment of a student performance should include both types

- They make explicit to students, parents, and administrators the criteria for student achievement

- They can be used by students to assess their own performance and the performance of other students

Depending on purposes and the standards being assessed, several different forms of rubrics are used by teachers. A report by the Council of Chief State School Officers (1995) defines three basic types—task specific, developmental, and relative—but there are variations and combinations. This report also identifies strengths and weaknesses. Examples of these three types are in Tables 6.6 through 6.10, and descriptions of their strengths and weaknesses are in Table 6.11.

I found the developmental type the most difficult to find a good sample for, but there are three examples here. The class participation checklist (Table 6.10) is from the seed germination unit described above. Table 6.7 is a developmental rubric based on the named, but not clearly defined, levels in the math scope and sequence discussed above. Only three developmental levels, attached to median grade level expectations, are described in the scope and sequence. Four levels with the top-level standard have been suggested as desirable. I believe that the top and fourth level in the case of the math concepts would be that the student is capable of applying the concept in creative ways.

For each concept as delineated in Table 6.7, the median expectation or standard of development for the grade level will be different. In essence, based on median expectations, each student can then be below, at, or above standard for each concept, but the expectations and the judgments are ordered by the developmental sequence for the concept. For example, a student may be at level 2 (concept mastery) of the developmental sequence, but the expectation for that grade is for her to be at level 3 (algorithmic mastery), and therefore the student is below standard. If scored grades are desired, the report could be adapted to provide a numerical equivalent for achievement of the standard, surpassing it or not achieving it, and the report would appear more like the simple developmental rubric in Table 6.9.

Although the examples of task-specific (Table 6.6) and relative (Table 6.8) rubrics may be easily shared with students, the negative descriptors may have to be changed. Additional adjustments would have to made in the developmental rubrics for this purpose. Children might respond to math levels called touching, touching and thinking, thinking without touching, and thinking of new ways.

TABLE 6.6 A Task-Specific Rubric

Skill	Above Standard	At Standard	Below Standard
Use of simple machines	Involves more than four kinds of machines	Involves three to four kinds of simple machines	Involves fewer than three kinds of machines
Understanding of simple machines	Can clearly and in detail explain how it works	Can generally explain how it works	Has difficulty explaining how it works
	Can clearly and in detail explain how it helps us do work	Can generally explain how it helps us do work	Has difficulty explaining how it helps us do work

SOURCE: Egeland (1997, p. 45).

TABLE 6.7 A Developmental Math Rubric

Explanation of Levels			
Level 1	Level 2	Level 3	Level 4
Procedural exploration: Can solve problems based on this concept using the real or concrete representative materials. But unable to explain concept	Concept mastery: Can solve problems and explain the concept used. May still need concrete material	Procedural or algorithmic mastery: Can generalize the concept and use it to solve problems without concrete material	Application mastery: Can generate an original problem using concept or apply it in an unusual way

Individual Assessment of Levels		
Concept	Expected Level for Grade	Student's Level
17. (See standard list)	Level 1	Level 2
18. (See standard list)	Level 2	Level 4

TABLE 6.8 A Relative Rubric: Language and Literacy

Skill	Exceeds Standard	At Standard	Below Standard
Listening			
Speaking			

TABLE 6.9 A Developmental Rubric: Language and Literacy—Grade One: Fall, Winter, Spring

		F	W	S
Listens for meaning in discussions and conversations	Not yet In process Proficient			
Speaks easily, conveying ideas in discussions and conversations	Not yet In process Proficient			

SOURCE: Adapted from Meisels (1996/1997, p. 60). Used with permission.

TABLE 6.10 A Developmental Rubric: Class Participation Criteria Checklist

Level	Speaking/Reasoning	Listening
4	Understands questions before answering Cites appropriate evidence from background information Expresses in complete thoughts Displays logic and insight Synthesizes ideas	Pays close attention and records details Responses include comments of others Identifies logical errors Overcomes distractions
3	Responds to questions voluntarily Comments indicate thought and reflection Ideas draw interest from others	Generally pays attention Responds thoughtfully to others Questions logical structures Self-absorption may distract the ideas of others
2	Responds when called upon Comments indicate little effort in preparation Comments may be illogical and may ignore important details Ideas may not relate to previous comments	Attention wavers Classifies ideas inappropriately Requires inordinate repetition of questions Shows interest in own ideas
1	Extremely reluctant to participate Comments are illogical and meaningless Has incomplete thoughts Makes little relationships between comments and text	Acts uninvolved in discussion Misinterprets previous comments and ideas Shows ambivalence toward any ideas presented

SOURCE: University of the State of New York, 1997.

TABLE 6.11 Rubrics: Comparing Types

Type	Strengths	Weaknesses
Task-specific	• High inter-rater agreement • Faster to learn • Direct measure of a task • Must develop, verify, and train a new rubric for each question or task	• Measures small part of a skill domain • Poor generalizability or transfer ability to other real world tasks • Doesn't indicate what to teach next
Developmental	• Increases understanding of what is meant by the concept and what to do next • Increases teaching to the skills • Direct measure of the skill • Can tell what is being assessed by looking at the rubric • Different rubrics do not have to be developed • Improved generalization of skills • Same examples can be used across different grade levels or groups	• May take longer to develop • Needs consensus from users on what skills come next • May be harder to learn but easier to use
Relative	• Fastest to learn • Good for the big picture • Will work for most accountability needs	• Can't always tell what is being assessed by looking at the rubric • Reliability is not always high • Rubric doesn't always help to define the concept • Dependent on different ex-examples, that is, anchor samples, at different grades, or for different target groups • Doesn't communicate to students what to do differently at different points in time

SOURCE: Council of Chief State School Officers (1995).

Challenge 4: Sharing Results With Students, Parents, and the Community

Many educators and parents are anxious about the shift toward more authentic assessment and grading. Teachers are overwhelmed by the complex task of developing rubrics that can be translated into grades. Although it seems much easier to describe levels of task-driven performance tests than it is to define developmental levels of constructs, as evidenced by the great variation in quality of the samples above, we have hardly developed mature skills in our new endeavors. Different audiences will require us to make different kinds of assessments. Reporting of the results and the consequences will vary. Reporting forms will need revision, and re-education of audiences may be necessary.

It will take time for students to develop skills and positive attitudes toward self- and peer assessments. Parents may need to be involved in the creation of new assessments, or at least informed of the systems and the standards they match before they get report cards. Some audiences will insist on familiar grades. Comparative grading seems to be built into our society, and many people feel uncomfortable without it. Almost any good set of scaled rubrics can be converted to grades. But audiences need to know how the qualitative basis of rubric-based grades can be used by the teacher to inform instruction, by the parent to provide guidance and motivation, and by the student to help plan the next step.

The community may be suspicious of changes from familiar patterns, especially those that avoid the wide-scale comparisons that make them secure in their investments in home and property. Parents and public officials may be reluctant to abandon their comfortable standardized tests. It may be necessary to reassure them with the most authentic version of a nationally or internationally normed test. New York has a plan for combinations of performance and conventional tests. The conventional tests will be given on demand rather than regularly. Teachers may also want to construct some traditional tests so that students are prepared for these.

Among the advantages of alternative assessments are that they cause us to focus clearly on what we wish to accomplish, and they can be more squarely situated as part of the instructional process. Changing assessment practices can help us do better, but there are some cautions as we progress in this endeavor. We should not allow formal assessments to overpower our other goals. We cannot forget the power of the informal measures that are an integral part of the discourse we have with our students and they have with each other. The true value of any assessment lies in its ability to promote the best possible learning environment.

Meg, Brad, and April have to plan for this environment and include assessment elements. Here are some things for them to consider after they complete the steps in Table 6.2.

- Identify which standards are mostly procedural or processes. These can usually be more easily generalized and yet individually assessed with a relative rubric.

- Identify major constructs or ideas that may be acquired gradually in a developmental sequence. These will require some developmental rubrics if you wish to measure progress levels through performance tasks. Once you have done that, use the construct levels to design a conventional test as well. Occasionally compare results.

- Engage students in the process of self-assessment as much as possible. Establish patterns such as journal writing and peer editing.

- Task-specific assessments may be most helpful if they are an integral part of enabling activities. Make them work for you and the students, but unless they are connected in some way to more general outcomes, it may be a waste of time to report these to distal audiences. Do not overuse them in the classroom environment because they may interfere with other student goals. No one wants to feel that everything done is constantly assessed. Try getting students to create them.

- Make personal reflection on the results of students' assessments a routine. Be a teacher-researcher. Take the time to do an analysis that compares results of different activities. Try to discover why some activities work better than others.

- Use technology wherever you can. Use a camcorder to provide data for you and feedback for other audiences. Consider constructing performance tasks that require the students to use a computer (e.g., a PowerPoint or Hyper Studio presentation), and that can then be saved on a file for you to see and respond to when you have time, or buy a program that does that, or have the students construct the tasks for each other. Grab ideas from other teachers over the Internet. Share your ideas with other teachers. Share them with me at pgsolomon@msn.com.

Notes

1. Standardized tests are designed to be administered under controlled and uniform conditions, including time allocations and support from

teachers and other materials. Standardized tests are usually *normed*. Normed tests are tests that have been administered to methodically selected sample populations (the norming sample). Scores reported for test takers are then comparatively based on the performance of participants in this sample.

2. A *juku* is an after-school intensive test preparation practice that many Japanese children attend regularly.

3. Test developers do sometimes offer item analyses that would be helpful, but they are not well used. Even criterion-referenced tests have not been adequately applied by teachers.

4. Computer-based forms of these commonly administered tests have not proven popular with students.

7

Where Do We Go From Here?

Although they had made some good progress with their project, and were having some fun doing it, Meg, Brad, and April soon realized that the task of writing a curriculum based on the new state science standards was indeed daunting. They were using the outline Brad had brought back from the summer workshop as a template, and the unit he had already produced with his working group fit right in with what they were planning. It was interpreting the standards themselves and matching them with activities that was difficult. "How do you do scientific analysis and interpretation of data in 3rd grade? I'm not sure even I can do that!" April wondered out loud to her colleagues. Brad responded by telling her about his experience at the summer workshop, where he had had an opportunity to try out some new-generation software at an IBM facility. "Well, the kids can collect data about the temperature each day with these probes that connect to a computer—or they can even use a special calculator." Meg loved the idea of kids going out to collect data, but was still somewhat confused about what the computer could do with the data once collected. She had always done data collection with her science kit. Her students made tables and graphs of the data they collected without using any technology except for a thermometer, a pencil, and a ruler.

One of the things that concerned them all was the fact that there were only a few computers in the whole school, and most of these were slow and able to use only the drill-and-practice software that was not exciting to the kids anymore. A recent budget referendum that would have gotten them new computers was turned down by the community. And they had lost out to a nearby city for some federal grant money for technology. "Do we have to use computer technology? Is that mandated by the state?" April asked. Perhaps they could find a way to get around the mandates. She remembered other times when they had ignored state curriculum guides. Brad then reminded them about the new performance tests based on the standards that their students would have to take. "I think it might be different this time," he said.

It needs to be different this time! The new millennium will bring changes in our culture and society that will require profoundly different approaches to education—and the children, for whom new technology is already as basic as the pencil and text were to us, will be different. They will have to survive and compete on a global basis with many others. This chapter is about what we need to do to build the curriculum bridge to the future.

Where Will the Leadership for Needed Change Come From?

President Clinton used the charismatic approach, not a new policy, in encouraging schools to participate voluntarily in his call for national tests based on national standards. Considering the differences of opinion discussed in Chapter 2, "Are New Standards Necessary?" I believe he made a wise move. Others may agree with me. After reviewing conclusions reached by researchers who studied how education had been influenced by the relationships between different levels of government over the past decade, Michael Kirst (1995) reports that "power and influence in education's intergovernmental relations is not a zero-sum game whereby one level gains and another loses the ability to influence policy" (p. 18). He suggests that new state curricular initiatives can "galvanize more local curriculum policy making and leadership at the local level, so that policy-making impact of all government levels can increase simultaneously" (p. 18). This is just as it happened in Brad, April, and Meg's case, and there is strong evidence that local school districts are responding broadly to the new policies at the state level.

Kirst (1995) proposes that even if the curriculum standards are in general form—most of the new state documents have been—they still can have an effect on practice by shaping attitudes about content and performance. He suggests that policymakers use a combination of push and pull factors to help implement new policies. *Push factors* include the mandated assessments and graduation requirements discussed in previous chapters. *Pull factors* include incentives such as grants and demonstrations of effective practice. Based on his interpretation of the data, Kirst admits, however, that state education agencies are not well structured or prepared to help implement systemic reform. He identifies local school central offices as similarly fragmented, with a lack of ability to work intensively on curriculum in all subjects at one time; in agreement with many others, Kirst identifies the need for teacher capacity building. His main conclusion is that policy can "create a skeleton or shell in which classroom practice can change" (p. 21). We need such a skeleton or shell to give better form to our restructuring efforts.

In related articles on systemic reform Cohen (1995) identifies the need for coherence in direction at all levels as a major problem and Corcoran and Goertz (1995) find the current systems fragmented and suggest that we need to address the total system's capacity to carry out reform. These needs were illustrated in the summer workshop that Brad attended. Everyone was confused by the terminology. Some of the state documents had been issued before the adoption of the nationally used terminology of content and performance standards. New documents combined the new terms with the old ones in unexplained ways. Many districts had recently written new curriculum using the outcome-based education terms and had different templates. Corcoran and Goertz identify inappropriate sequencing of implementation as a common problem, but some of the teachers in Brad's workshop also reported that central office and building administrators had different opinions on whether or not the new standards were worthwhile. Because of this lack of coherence, teachers receive fragmented messages and policies are implemented with great variation.

Cohen identifies teachers (and their administrators) as both the problem and the solution, and urges us to look at teachers' professional development and instructional practice if we wish to change instruction. Even if policy becomes more coherent, "coherence in policy is not the same thing as coherence in practice" (p. 16). Corcoran and Goertz suggest that we look more broadly at "the quality and quantity of the resources available for teaching" (p. 27), which I have defined as enabling standards, and more carefully at "exaggerated claims about the effectiveness of various strategies" (p. 30). Although these authors identify the problems and make valid recommendations for overcoming the identified impediments to systemic reform, they offer little in the way of suggestions for leadership to provide coherence for either policy or practice.

Teacher Professional Development

Many researchers have identified the professional development of teachers as the key to educational reform. They have also recognized that professional development is not an easy task. Little (1993) explains that, although traditional forms of delivery of professional development might work for the skills training components of reform, especially if transfer of knowledge from experts is followed up with opportunities to practice and is supported by coaching, presently called for reforms go beyond skills. They require that persons in local situations grapple with what broad principles look like in practice. Little quotes Deborah Meier[1] as saying that these reforms require us to reinvent teaching and schooling. This is exactly what Brad's curriculum writing team was struggling with. The teachers could easily write daily lesson plans, but they had great difficulty connecting lessons to the broad commencement standard that "students will use mathematical analysis, scientific inquiry, and engineering design, as appropriate, to pose questions, seek answers, and develop solutions" (University of the State of New York, 1996, 1997).

Teachers need intensive professional development programs to help them accomplish this reinvention. Designing a curriculum down from a commencement content standard, constructing matching content and performance standards, and then assessing them in alternative forms at one's grade level are new, demanding, and very different tasks. Understanding and implementing a constructivist approach to teaching is a departure from the way most of us learned in school. Dealing with multiple intelligences and student goals and building classroom dialogues that encourage metacognitive strategies and generalizations at the algorithmic level require us to learn and practice all the new knowledge available. Just reading about these new ideas may not be enough. Like our students, we must construct new concepts. Time for interactive reflection with our peers and time for guided practice may be necessary.

Why would teachers bother to participate in professional development that will help them learn these challenging new techniques? Stout (1997) identifies some motives that have encouraged them in the past.

- Salary enhancement: Eligibility to compete for extra increments or to climb a career ladder is often tied to participation in staff development.

- Certificate maintenance: New York recently suggested such a policy.

- Career mobility: Teachers take courses and degrees and participate in workshops to build resumes. Having done so, they attempt to leave education for other occupations or to pursue other careers within education, administration being the notable example.

Stout (1997) maintains that none of these three motives, in itself, necessarily leads to better performance by teachers because existing systems do nothing to ensure or encourage it. He believes that a fourth motive, the intrinsic wish to gain new skills and knowledge to enhance one's own classroom performance, offers the greatest promise. I disagree with Stout's minimization of the existence of this motive. I believe that the vagueness he sees in teachers' commitment is because the extrinsic rewards of the first three motives have clouded the issue, and teachers have not been given the venues in which to develop intrinsic goals. I harken back to the discussion of gold stars versus intrinsic goals in Chapter 5, "Constructing Creative Classrooms," when I suggest that we should give this approach a chance for teachers as well. I have seen teachers' intrinsic goals at work for close to a half century in my own engagement as an educator in many different roles. And as I describe below, I saw them again last summer. I do agree with Stout that this fourth motive is the critical one, and I agree that programs that engage teachers more directly in plans for overall school improvement have a greater potential for success.

If intrinsic motivation to improve one's own performance is to take over from the other three motives, the nature of traditional engagement of teachers in professional development may need a whole new approach. Smylie (1996) identifies some best practices in professional development that have worked. They resemble the things that work with students. They have "a focus on the concrete tasks of day-to-day work" (p. 10) and opportunities to learn that are grounded in inquiry, experimentation, and reflection. They involve interaction with other teachers, and are coherent, intensive, and ongoing. We may need to get away from the present marketplace concept of professional development for teachers in which competing graduate programs are disconnected from real needs, and from the one-shot conference days and haphazard inservice programs of single districts. Networking offers this promise. It may also offer a new and different form of leadership.

Teacher Networks

Teacher networks have appeared in several different forms. There are privately funded and university affiliated networks such as the New Standards Project and the Center for Research on Evaluation, Standards, and Student Testing (CRESST). Other successful networks include the Philadelphia Alliance for Teaching Humanities in the Schools (PATHS), the Urban Mathematics Collaboratives, and the Bay Area Writing Project. The strength of these groups is based on several aspects that include capacity for teacher support over and above the district or university, norms of informed experimentation, a system of mutual aid (mentoring) that compensates for uneven preparation of teachers, connections to the classroom, and engagement of teachers in professional discussion and debate (Little, 1993).

After a study of networks that are part of the National Center for Restructuring Education, Schools, and Teaching, Ann Lieberman (1996) reports that the opportunity for sharing among teacher participants "has the effect of dignifying and giving shape to the substance of educators' experiences. . . . Networks are particularly good at helping school-based educators discuss and work on current problems . . . teachers and administrators find it easier to question, ask for help, or tell it like it is" (p. 52). She describes leadership in networks as making phone calls, raising money, arranging meetings, brokering resources and people, and negotiating time commitments for university and school-based educators.

Lieberman (1996) is right on the mark! That is exactly what I had to do to bring about the McExtend network's summer workshop that Brad attended. This latest endeavor began with a phone call to district administrators inviting them to attend a breakfast meeting at a local diner. The meeting led to a successful Goals 2000 grant application and a sizable extension of previous networking activities.

Our network started as an outreach from a college graduate education program to the surrounding schools. As the Marie Curie Math and Science Center, our first agenda was in math, science, and technology education; we provided inservice support and an enrichment program for secondary students.[2] With increased funding, however, the network activities have expanded beyond these subjects. The network has several important distinguishing characteristics.

- An advisory board comprising school district administrators, teachers, parents, students, college faculty, and industry representatives.

- Peer coaching in the inservice programs—teachers learn how to engender trust and interact with each other for the purpose of instructional improvement. In most cases they must sign up with colleagues. The districts recruit participants in what we call peer interactive partnerships (PIPs). A PIP is made up of an experienced teacher and a novice.

- Connections between the program elements. Teacher participants in the inservice programs practice in the secondary student program. It becomes a learning laboratory. Follow-up on-site reflective meetings are held in the districts with college faculty, participants, and building administrators. Experienced teachers who participate are also eligible to become paid supervisors for student teachers.

- Team teaching in the student program—most often a team of scientists and teachers, but sometimes a pair of teachers.

- Cooperation with local industry. Local businesses have provided us with venues, materials, and personnel for the student and teacher programs.

Our network is much smaller than the ones mentioned above, but we are now entering our 8th year. As Project McExtend (an extension of the original Marie Curie Center program), we include all the school districts within an entire county, local teachers centers, and the college. Our support comes from some private sources, the districts, the college, and the state (using federal sources), and we are accountable to each policy-making entity to some degree, but essentially we have designed our agenda, shared it, and received approval.

For the current Goals 2000 component, there is a leadership team that has three district-based teachers and two college faculty members. The leadership team planned every detail of the program, prepared the instructional staff, and led the working groups. Our instructional staff for the summer workshop included eight district teachers, two principals, three college faculty members, two outside consultants, and a scientist at a local research facility. Our participants included 119 K through 12 teachers and 10 college faculty.

Based on a study of state-supported teacher networks, Firestone and Pennell (1997) present three propositions that offer suggestions for the design of networks. I will use our Marie Curie and McExtend experience as confirmation, elaboration, or correction of these propositions.

- Proposition 1: Capacity-building networks contribute more directly to teacher learning, motivation, and empowerment than do policy-supporting networks.

Although most of our program has involved capacity building, this summer's venture included policy support as well. Teachers need to be informed of their responsibilities toward meeting the standards and they need the capacity to deal with them and the new technology the standards demand. It may be a good idea to combine the two. The discomfort we observed in the beginning was with accepting and understanding the standards, and with the requirement for a product of written curriculum that matched them. A few participants had a hard time accepting this responsibility, probably because of previous, less rigorous staff development experiences. After they got going, they were all fine. Like Brad, most participants not only enjoyed the technology components but immediately worked some of them into their curriculum units.

- Proposition 2: Extrinsic incentives can attract teachers, but teachers are most likely to continue participating when they receive the intrinsic incentives that come from learning that is useful in the classroom.

McExtend provides monetary incentives in the form of stipends, but these rarely match regular pay. Another incentive is the possibility of getting graduate credit at a reduced cost, which can then be used as Stout (1997) defines. Less than half the teachers in this summer's program opted for this, and these represent the novices in the PIPs who needed the credits. Even though some teachers complained at first about having to work in groups to write their own curriculum units (a task they had previously viewed as an isolated one), they ended up loving the opportunity to share the experience with colleagues outside their districts, creating higher quality products, and implementing them with great success.

- Proposition 3: Networks reach a greater variety of teachers by offering a mix of constructivist and directive activities.

We have done just that! A formal program in classroom management techniques based on Saphier and Gower's (1997) skillful teacher approach began with a more directive course (with nondirective activities embedded), but it was followed by specific time for interaction back at the home school. It was in this time that teachers intersubjectively constructed new knowledge (see Chapter 3, "What We Now Know About How Learning Happens"). The curriculum writing challenge this summer began with 4 days of direct instruction (from many of their colleagues). It was followed by 4 days spread out over 4 months for them to interact with their working group and try their units with their students.

Assessments of achievement of the content standards planned for the teachers in previous programs were based on self-assessment questionnaires and follow-up interviews with them and their principals during the following year as they practiced what they had learned. They show growth in the use of the particular skills, but even greater all around influence on their professional relationships with colleagues. This is of significant value in that it sets the stage for long-term improvement. The evidence for the curriculum experience is still being gathered, but preliminary feedback demonstrates similar or even better effect.

Teacher Networks as Leaders

The real evidence for the leadership value of teacher networks is in the long-term improvement of practice and in the consequent improved achievement of students; that remains to be measured. I disagree, however, with one of Firestone and Pennell's (1997) conclusions. They state that most teachers are not ready for challenging instruction or complex thinking about instruction, and they would benefit more from direct instruction. Thinking such as this is tantamount to having low expectations for students and then having them realized. High standards mean high standards for teachers as well, and this means giving them greater responsibility for complex thinking and decision making. Ready or not, they must face the challenge of learning how to provide this kind of instruction for their students, and this is the model we should use for them!

Teacher networks can help teachers overcome the fragmentation that exists between schools and districts and between schools and higher education institutions. Given the right policy support, networks can also relieve the burden of overextended state education and central office personnel. A word of caution, however, is that the network must be seen as part of the overall district staff development program, not as a separate entity. Its efforts must be integrated into whatever is happening on a local level. I have tried to deal with this potential problem by maintaining close contact with state- and district-level policymakers and demonstrating the quality of our efforts. For example, Brad came to the McExtend program at the suggestion of his principal to prepare for the curriculum work with April and Meg. He came back with ideas and shared knowledge and a template for beginning his design that reflected a common vocabulary that reached beyond his own setting—and made his work assume greater importance and prestige. As noted above, we also try to limit our program instructional staff to all levels of network participants. But I think the following personal anecdote provides another aspect of the value of teachers learning together and the value of networks.

*   *   *

Kathy and John came in to my office today. Kathy is a biology teacher (and new department chair) at a network high school. John is a professor of biology at the college. Both had worked in the Marie Curie program for secondary students, but they did not really know each other until they joined the same working group this summer. I had earlier asked Kathy to join us in the kids program again, but she had hesitated because of her new responsibilities.

At this moment in time, these teachers might both be unrecognizable to their students. They were covered in mud! Their curriculum writing had taken them to a nearby stream to find out what was in there for their students to find. They were quite animated, and joked with each other about a big fish and turtle that almost nipped Kathy's leg. Spontaneously, they blurted out how much fun it had been to work on this project together—and to my surprise, suggested that they could team up and try their new curriculum units with the kids on Saturday mornings.

*   *   *

The McExtend curriculum units and the relationships formed may take us into even greater opportunities for learning by sharing. The units will be posted on a Web page for the benefit of teachers all over the world. This brings us to another kind of network and another promise for the future.

Using Technology and Its Networks for Building Curriculum

In an e-mail message to me, Belinda Hill defined the Internet as an unexplored region and a border between countries, an "electronic frontier." She quotes Barlow's (1991, p. 19) definition of it as

> a place where trespassers leave no footprints, where goods can be stolen an infinite number of times and yet remain in possession of their original owners, where businesses you never heard of can own the home, where the physics is that of thought rather than things, and where everyone is as virtual as the shadows in Plato's cave.

This definition can remind us of the great possibilities of technology as a tool and a component of curriculum. It also warns us of possible dangers.

Let us begin with the notion of technology as a place for the physics of thought. This does not describe the first-generation software that is in place in many schools today. This software was a replication of print materials. It did have an advantage over print materials, however, in its immediate feedback and student control components. It fed students' needs for interest, self-efficacy, and intrinsic goals. It was that kind of motivation that produced the current generation of technology users. Although this software has been in use in schools for over a decade, it has never really been integrated into the curriculum. Like dittos from an extra workbook, the software programs were add-ons that the kids seemed to like.

The advent of CD-ROMs, with their multimedia potential for interactive engagement of the learner, not only heightened the previous motivational advantages for students, but also introduced some of the physics that Barlow (1991) talks about. If students have to make choices about how to design an airship that they can then race, they face a different and more constructive challenge. The Internet has expanded this potential exponentially. If students can use their programs to access scientific data banks directly to help them make predictions about earthquakes or sunspots, they are beyond a level that any traditional classroom with the best possible teacher can provide. If they use their programs to communicate visually and individually with the scientists who collected this data, they are reaching beyond the still-necessary human interactions of their own cooperative groups. If they use computer-interfaced environmental probes, wind tunnels, and bridge constructions to gather environmental data and make original designs, not only have they used technology as a tool to learn something that is already in the consensual domain (Chapter 3, "What We Now Know About How Learning Happens"), they have used it to create completely new knowledge.

This potential extends beyond the science classroom. If 2nd graders can write their book reports and design their PowerPoint presentations so that others will want to read their reports, they have reached a new level of communication skill. If social studies classes can maintain ongoing communications with students from all over the world, get original geographic and economic data from data banks in the countries they are studying or original transcripts of congressional discussions, and then use these communications and information to simulate new situations and make decisions, they are doing something my teachers never dreamed of.

Today's teachers can no longer dream, they must prepare for this. The same possibility for new knowledge exists for them. As Barlow (1991) suggests, they can steal. The Web offers much that can be helpful to teachers. From their own classrooms or home computer, they can access curriculum documents and samples that teachers have produced all over the world. They can discuss them with the writers and with other colleagues who have used them. Their discussions make the owner or originator feel a sense of efficacy (they can count the hits), and perhaps inspire the users to return the sharing favor. Preservice teachers (and experienced teachers) practicing in the field in a rural environment can access these materials and communicate regularly with professors and classmates back at their faraway institutions.

Technology for Communicating With Our Public

Technology can help us do a better job of communicating with parents and the public. It can also bring us help from others. Parents with computers no longer need to ask, "What did you do today?" if they can get an on-line report from the teacher. Many schools and classes now have Web pages where students can post and share their work. Students out ill can get assignments and interact with classmates back at school. The school district in which I live has many students who come from economically deprived homes without computers. We plan to put computers in community centers and local businesses that want to help with access for the children. The libraries and churches already have them. We also plan for a volunteer corps of community on-line homework helpers. Greater involvement by these individuals may engender greater knowledge of what we do; greater trust in our efforts may be the unexpected result. School report cards on-line may still be requested, but reading students' stories and viewing their artwork may be more convincing and more meaningful. We will have to be careful what we send, however!

This brings me to another piece of Barlow's (1991) definition: the virtual nature of the Internet. We all have to learn new information filtering skills, skills that were always necessary but are more so now that the forms of communication are so expanded. We need to learn how to evaluate what others say. We cannot accept everything on the Internet as truth. It doesn't have a librarian to help screen the stuff we see. Because it is virtual, teachers still need to make the decisions about when and how to use technologically based experiences and information, and we still need the human social learning requirement of face-to-face interaction with other human beings. Even the techies flock to computer conferences, and my computer scientist daughter prefers a phone call to e-mail. Most students prefer to have a friend at their side as they explore the world with their computers. Brad, April, and Meg can read this book and access the standards of many states and the curriculum units of many teachers including those in our network. But as they implement the standards that others may have agreed on and they have been given responsibility for, they will still need to use spoken words; smiles of understanding, approval, and satisfaction; quizzical looks of confusion; and other human exchanges as they learn with each other and with their students across the curriculum bridge.

Notes

1. Deborah Meier is the principal of the Central Park East School in New York City. The school has been very successful using a restructured curriculum and alternative assessments with diverse populations of students.

2. The Marie Curie program is validated by the state of New York for dissemination purposes.

References

Allan, S. D. (1991). Ability grouping research reviews: What do they say about grouping and the gifted? *Educational Leadership, 48*(6), 60-74.

American Association for the Advancement of Science. (1989). *2061: Science for all Americans.* Washington, DC: Author.

American Association for the Advancement of Science. (1994). *Benchmarks for science literacy.* Washington, DC: Author.

Anderman, E. M., & Maehr, M. L. (1994). Motivation and schooling in the middle grades. *Review of Educational Research, 64*(2), 287-309.

Anderson, J. R. (1983). *The architecture of cognition.* Cambridge, MA: Harvard University Press.

Anderson, J. R. (1990). *The adaptive character of thought.* Hillsdale, NJ: Lawrence Erlbaum.

Anderson, J. R., Reder, L. M., & Simon, H. A. (1996). Situated learning and education. *Educational Researcher, 25*(4), 5-11.

Anderson, J. R., Reder, L. M., & Simon, H. A. (1997). Rejoinder: Situated versus cognitive perspectives: Form versus substance. *Educational Researcher, 26*(1), 18-21.

Ausubel, D. P. (1963). *The psychology of meaningful learning.* New York: Grune & Stratton.

Ausubel, D. P. (1968). *Educational psychology: A cognitive view.* New York: Holt, Rhinehart & Winston.

Bailey, S. M. (1996). Shortchanging boys and girls. *Educational Leadership, 53*(8), 75-79.

Baker, D. F. (1997). Response: Good news bad news, and international comparisons: Comment on Bracey. *Educational Researcher, 26*(3), 16-17.

Ball, D. L., & Cohen, D. K. (1996). Reform by the book: What is—or might be—the role of curriculum materials in teacher learning and instructional reform. *Educational Researcher, 25*(9), 6-8, 14.

Barlow, J. P. (1991). Coming into the country. *Communications of the ACM, 34*(3), 19-21.

Berliner, D. C., & Biddle, B. J. (1995). *The manufactured crisis: Myths, fraud and the attack on America's public schools.* Reading, MA: Addison Wesley.

Blakesley, S. (1995, March 21). How the brain might work: A new theory of consciousness. *New York Times,* pp. C1, C10.

Borthwick, A., & Nolan K. (1996). Performance standards: How good is good enough. *Pre-Summit Briefing Materials: 1996 National Education Summit.* Palisades, NY: Governors' Commission Report for New Standards.

Bracey, G. W. (1996). International comparisons and the condition of American education. *Educational Researcher, 25*(1), 5-11.

Bracey, G. W. (1997). On comparing the incomparable: A response to Baker and Stedman. *Educational Researcher, 26*(3), 19-26.

Bruer, J. T. (1997). Education and the brain: A bridge too far. *Educational Researcher, 26*(8), 4-16.

Bryant, A., & Houston, P. (1997). The roles of superintendent and school board in engaging the public with public schools. *Kappan, 78*(10), 756-759.

Canady, R. L., & Rettig, M. D. (1995). The power of innovative scheduling. *Educational Leadership, 53*(3), 4-10.

Carpenter, T. P., et al. (1994, April). *Teaching mathematics for learning and understanding in the primary grades.* Paper presented to the American Educational Research Association, New Orleans.

Cattell, R. B. (1963). Theory of fluid and crystallized intelligence: A critical experiment. *Journal of Educational Psychology, 54,* 1-22.

Checkley, K. (1997). The first seven and the eighth: A conversation with Howard Gardner. *Educational Leadership, 55*(1), 8-13.

Chin, C., & Brewer, W. F. (1993). The role of anomalous data in knowledge acquisition: A theoretical framework and implications for science instruction. *Review of Educational Research, 63*(1), 1-49.

Chubb, J. E., & Moe, T. M. (1990). *Politics, markets, and America's schools.* Washington, DC: Brookings Institution.

Cobb, P. (1990). Multiple perspectives. In L. P. Steffe & T. Wood (Eds.), *Transforming children's mathematics education: International perspectives* (pp. 200-215). Hillsdale, NJ: Lawrence Erlbaum.

Cohen, D. K. (1995). What is the system in systemic reform? *Educational Researcher, 24*(9), 11-17.

Cohen, E. G. (1994). Restructuring the classroom: Conditions for productive small groups. *Review of Educational Research, 64*(1), 1-35.

Cohen, E. G., & Lotan, R. A. (1995). Producing equal status interaction in the heterogeneous classroom. *American Educational Research Journal, 32*(1), 99-121.

Cooper, H., & Dorr, N. (1995). Race comparisons on need for achievement: A meta-analytic alternative to Graham's narrative review. *Review of Educational Research, 65*(4), 483-508.

Corcoran, T., & Goertz, M. (1995). Instructural capacity and high performance standards. *Educational Researcher, 24*(9), 27-31.

Council for Basic Education. (1996). *History in the making: An independent review of the voluntary national history standards.* Washington, DC: Author.

Council of Chief State School Officers. (1995). *State collaborative on assessment and student standards year-end report.* Washington, DC: Author.

Darling-Hammond, L. (1990). Instructional policy into practice: The power of the bottom over the top. *Educational Evaluation and Policy Analysis, 12*(3), 233-241.

Doll, W. P. (1993). *A post-modern perspective on curriculum.* New York: Teachers College Press.

Dossey, J. A., Mullis, I. V. S., Lindquist, M. M., & Chambers, D. L. (1988). *The mathematics report card: Are we measuring up?* Princeton, NJ: Educational Testing Service.

Dweck, C. S., & Leggett, E. L. (1988). A social-cognitive approach to motivation and personality. *Psychological Review, 95,* 256-273.

Edmonds, R. R. (1983). Programs of school improvement: An overview. *Educational Leadership, 40*(4), 4-11.

Edwards, C. E. (1995). The 4x4 plan. *Educational Leadership, 53*(3), 16-19.

Egeland, P. (1997). Pulleys, planes and student performance. *Educational Leadership, 54*(4), 41-45.

Elmore, R. F. (1983). Complexity and control: What legislators and administrators can do about implementing policy. In L. S. Shulman & G. Sykes (Eds.), *Handbook of teaching and policy.* New York: Longman.

Elmore, R. F. (1987). Reform and the culture of authority in schools. *Educational Administration Quarterly, 23,* 6078.

Firestone, W. A., & Pennell, J. R. (1997). Designing state sponsored teacher networks: A comparison of two cases. *American Educational Research Journal, 34*(2), 237-266.

Fullan, M. (1982). *The meaning of educational change.* New York: Teachers College Press.

Fullan, M. (1990). Staff development, innovation, and institutional development. In Bruce Joyce (Ed.), *Changing school cultures through staff development* (pp. 3-25). Alexandria, VA: Association for Supervision and Curriculum Development.

Fuson, K., Wearne, D., Hiebert, J, Murray, H., Human, P., Olivier, A, Carpenter, T. P., & Fennema, E. (1997). Children's conceptual structures for multi-digit numbers and methods of multi-digit addition and subtraction. *Journal for Research in Mathematics Education, 28*(2), 130-162.

Gardner, H. (1983). *Frames of mind: The theory of multiple intelligences.* New York: Basic Books.

Gardner, H. (1993). *Multiple intelligences: The theory in practice.* New York: Basic Books.

Gardner, H. (1995). Multiple intelligences: Myths and messages. *Kappan, 77*(3), 202-209.

George, J. (1995). A loft-y idea for learning. *Educational Leadership, 53*(3), 56-57.

Ginsburg, H. P. (1981). The development of knowledge concerning written arithmetic. *International Journal of Psychology, 16*, 13-34.

Ginsburg, H. P. (1989). *Children's arithmetic: How they learn it and how you teach it.* Austin, TX: Pro-Ed.

Glass, S. R. (1997). Markets & myths: Autonomy in public and private schools. *Educational Education Policy Analysis Archives, 5*(1). [On-line.] Available: http://olam.ed.asu.edu/epaa/.

Glasser, W. (1986). *Control theory in the classroom.* New York: Harper & Row.

Graham, S. (1995). Narrative versus meta-analytic studies of race differences in motivation. *Review of Educational Research, 65*(4), 509-517.

Greene, S., & Ackerman, J. M. (1995). Expanding the constructivist metaphor: A rhetorical perspective on literacy research and practice. *Review of Educational Research, 65*(4), 383-420.

Greeno, J. G. (1997). Response on claims that answer the wrong questions. *Educational Research, 26*(1), 5-17.

Gutwillig, R. (1996, June 24). Kids, teachers offer thoughts on education. *Rockland Journal News,* p. 5.

Hatenbach, D. L., Ott, J., & Clark, S. (1996/1997). Performance based education in Aurora. *Educational Leadership, 54*(4), 51-55.

Heid, M. K. (1988). Resequencing skills and concepts in applied calculus using the computer as a tool. *Journal for Research in Mathematics Education, 19*(1), 3-25.

Herman, J. L., Aschbacher, P. R., & Winters, L. (1992). *A practical guide to alternative assessment.* Alexandria, VA: Association for Supervision and Curriculum Development.

Hoff, D. J. (1997, February 12). Clinton gives top billing to education plan. *Education Week on the Web.* [On-line]. Available: www. edweek.org.

Horn, J. L. (1985). Remodeling old models of intelligence. In B. B. Wolman (Ed.), *Handbook of intelligence* (pp. 267-300). New York: John Wiley.

House, E. R. (1996). A framework for appraising educational reforms. *Educational Researcher, 25*(7), 6-14.

Immerwahr, J., & Johnson, J. (1996). Americans' views on standards. In *Pre-Summit Briefing Materials: 1996 National Education Summit.* Palisades, NY: Governors' Commission Report.

Japan Society of Mathematical Education. (1990). Excerpts from mathematics program in Japan. In *Pre-Summit Briefing Materials: 1996 National Education Summit.* Palisades, NY: Governors' Commission Report for New Standards.

Johnson, D. W., & Johnson R. T. (1989). *Cooperation and competition: Theory and research.* Edina, MN: Interaction.

Johnson, D. W., Johnson R. T., & Holubec, E. J. (1987). *Revised circles of learning: Cooperation in the classroom.* Edina, MN: Interaction.

Joyce, B., & Weil, M. (1996). *Models of teaching.* Boston: Allyn & Bacon.

Kirst, M. W. (1995). Recent research in intergovernmental relations in education. *Educational Researcher, 24*(9), 18-22.

Kohn, A. (1993). *Punished by rewards: The trouble with gold stars, incentive plans, A's, praise, and other bribes.* Boston: Houghton Mifflin.

Kohn, A. (1996). By all available means: Cameron & Pierce's defense of extrinsic motivators. *Review of Educational Research, 66*(1), 1-4.

Labaree, D. F. (1997). Public goods, private goods: The American struggle over educational goals. *American Educational Research Journal, 34*(1), 39-81.

Lehmann, S., & Spring, E. (1996). High academic standards and school reform: Education leaders speak out. In *Pre-Summit Briefing Materials: 1996 National Education Summit.* Palisades, NY: Governors' Commission Report for New Standards.

Lepper, M. R., Keavney, M., & Drake, M. (1996). Extrinsic motivation and intrinsic rewards: A commentary on Cameron and Pierce's meta-analysis. *Review of Educational Research, 66*(1), 33-38.

Lerman, S. (1996). Intersubjectivity in mathematics learning: A challenge to the radical constructivist paradigm? *Journal for Research in Mathematics Education, 27*(2), 133-150.

Lezotte, L. W. (1981). Search for and description of characteristics of effective elementary schools: Lansing public schools. In R. R. Edmonds (Ed.), *A report on the research project: Search for effective schools* (pp. 6-15). East Lansing: Michigan State University.

Lieberman, A. (1996). Creating learning communities. *Educational Leadership, 54*(3), 51-55.

Little, J. W. (1993). Teachers' professional development in a climate of educational reform. *Educational Evaluation and Policy Analysis, 15*(2), 129-151.

Lohman, D. F. (1989). Human intelligence: An introduction to advancers in theory and research. *Review of Educational Research, 59*(4), 333-373.

Longstreet, W. S., & Shane, H. G. (1993). *Curriculum for a new millennium.* Needham, MA: Allyn & Bacon.

Lou, Y., Abrami, P. C., Spence, J. C., Poulsen, C., Chambers, B., & D'Appolina, S. (1996). Within-class grouping: A meta-analysis. *Review of Educational Research, 66*(4), 423-458.

Madaus, G., West, M. M., Harmon, M. C., Lomax, R. G., Viator, K. A., Mungal, C. F., Butler, P. A., McDowell, C., & Simmons, E. (1992). *The influence of testing on teaching math and science in grades 4-12.* Boston: Boston College, Center for the Study of Testing, Evaluation, and Educational Policy.

Mann, D., MacLaughlin, M. W., Baer, M., Greenwood, P. W., Prusoff, L., Wirt, J., & Zelman, G. (1975). *Federal programs supporting education change.* Santa Monica, CA: RAND Corp.

Marzano, R., Brandt, R., Hughes, S., Jones, B. F., Presseisen, B. Z., Rankin, S., & Suhor, C. (1988). *Thinking: A framework for curriculum and instruction.* Alexandria, VA: Association for Supervision and Curriculum Development.

Mayer, R. E., Sims, V., & Tajika, H. (1995). A comparison of how textbooks teach mathematical problem solving in Japan and the United States. *American Educational Research Journal, 32*(2), 443-460.

McCaslin, M. (1996). The problem of problem representation: The summit's conception of student. *Educational Researcher, 25*(8), 13-15.

McInerny, D. M, Roche, L., McInerny, V., & Marsh, H. (1997). Cultural perspectives on school motivation: The relevance and application of goal theory. *American Educational Research Journal, 34*(1), 207-236.

McNight, C. C., Grosswith, F. J., Dossey, J. A., Kifer, E., Swafford, J. O., Trevers, K. J., & Cooney, T. J. (1987). *The underachieving curriculum: Assessing U.S. school mathematics from an international perspective.* Champaign, IL: Stipes.

McREL Institute. (1993). *Conference materials.* Aurora, CO: Mid Continent Regional Educational Laboratory.

McTighe, J. (1996/1997). What happens between assessments? *Educational Leadership, 54*(4) 6-12.

Meisels, S. J. (1996/1997). Using work sampling in authentic assessments. *Educational Leadership, 54*(4), 60-65.

Messick, S. (1994). The interplay of evidence and consequences in the validation of performance assessments. *Educational Researcher, 23*(2), 13-23.

Mosle, S. (1996a, September 12). Scores count. *New York Times Magazine,* pp. 41-45.

Mosle, S. (1996b, October 27). The answer is national standards. *New York Times Magazine,* pp. 44-47.

Nash, J. M. (1997, February 3). Fertile minds. *Time.*

National Art Education Association. (1994). *A priority for reaching high standards.* Reston, VA: Author.

National Commission on Excellence in Education. (1983). *A nation at risk.* Washington, DC: U.S. Department of Education.

National Council for Social Studies. (1994). *Curriculum standards for the social studies: Expectations of excellence.* Washington, DC: Author.

National Council of Teachers of Mathematics, Commission on Standards for School Mathematics. (1989). *Curriculum and evaluation standards for school mathematics.* Reston, VA: Author.

National Education Commission on Time and Learning. (1994). *Prisoners of time.* Washington, DC: Government Printing Office.

National Governors' Association. (1996). Education, standards, assessment and accountability in the states. In *Pre-Summit Briefing Materials: 1996 National Education Summit.* Palisades, NY: Governors' Commission Report for New Standards.

National Research Council. (1996). *National science education standards.* Washington, DC: National Academy Press.

Natriello, G. (1996). Diverting attention from conditions in American schools. *Educational Researcher, 25*(8), 7-9.

New Jersey Education Association. (1996, March). Commentary: Making the standards work. *NJEA Review,* p. 76.

New York State School Boards Association. (1990). *School boards & curriculum: Special focus on science and mathematics—A position paper.* Albany: Author.

Nichols, P. D. (1994). A framework for developing cognitively diagnostic assessments. *Review of Educational Research, 64*(4), 575-603.

O'Day, J., & Smith, M. S. (1993). Systemic reform and educational opportunity. In S. H. Fuhrman (Ed.), *Designing coherent school policy* (pp. 250-306). San Francisco: Jossey Bass.

Ogawa, R. T. (1994). The institutional sources of educational reform: The case of school-based management. *American Educational Research Journal, 31*(3), 519-548.

Orton, R. E. (1995). Ockham's razor and Plato's beard. *Journal for Research in Mathematics Education, 26*(3), 204-229.

Pajares, F. (1996). Self-efficacy beliefs in academic settings. *Review of Educational Research, 66*(4), 543-578.

Peeno, L. N. (1995). *Status of arts in the states.* Reston, VA: National Art Education Association.

Piaget, J. (1926). *The language and thought of the child.* New York: Harcourt Brace.

Piaget, J. (1977). *The development of thought: Equilibration of cognitive structures.* New York: Viking.

Pintrich, P. R., Marx, R. W., & Boyle, R. A. (1993). Beyond cold conceptual change: The role of motivational beliefs and contextual factors in the process of conceptual change. *Review of Educational Research, 63*(2), 167-169.

Purdie, N., & Hattie, J. (1996). Cultural differences in the use of strategies for self-regulated learning. *American Educational Research Journal, 33*(4), 845-872.

Qin, Z., Johnson, D., & Johnson, R. (1995). Cooperation, competition, and problem solving. *Review of Educational Research, 65*(2), 129-143.

Resnick, L. B. (1983). A developmental theory of number understanding. In H. Ginsburg (Ed.), *The development of mathematical thinking* (pp. 110-149). New York: Academic.

Resnick, L. B. (1989). *Education and learning.* Pittsburgh: University of Pittsburgh Learning, Research and Development Center.

Resnick, L. B., & Resnick, D. (1989). *Tests as standards of achievement in schools: The uses of standardized tests in American education.* Princeton, NJ: Educational Testing Service.

Review of Educational Research. (1993). Comments in reference to Wang et al. *Review of Educational Research, 63*(3), 295-364.

Reynolds, D. S., Doran, R. L., Allers, R. H., & Agruso, S. A. (1996). *Alternative assessment in sciences: A teacher's guide.* Buffalo, NY: State Education Department.

Rogers, H., & Saklofske, D. H. (1985). Self concepts, locus of control, and performance expectations of learning disabled children. *Journal of Learning Disabilities, 18,* 273-277.

Rosenshine, B., & Meister, C. (1994). Reciprocal teaching: A review of the research. *Review of Educational Research, 64*(4), 479-530.

Rosko, K. (1996). When two heads are better than one. *Journal of Teacher Education, 47*(2), 120-129.

Ryan, R., & Deci, E. L. (1996). When paradigms clash: Comments on Cameron and Pierce's claim that rewards do not undermine intrinsic motivation. *Review of Educational Research, 66*(1), 33-38.

Saphier, J., & Gower, R. (1997). *The skillful teacher.* Carlisle, MA: Research for Better Teaching.

Sarason, S. B. (1983). *Schooling in America.* New York: Free Press.

Sarason, S. B. (1990). *The predictable failure of educational reform.* San Francisco: Jossey Bass.

Sarason, S. B. (1993). *The case for change.* San Francisco: Jossey Bass.

Schmidt, W., McNight, C., & Raizen, S., in collaboration with six others. (1996). *A splintered vision: An investigation of U.S. science and mathematics education, executive summary.* Lansing: Michigan State University, U.S. National Research Center for the Third International Mathematics and Science Study.

Sedlak, M. W., Wheeler, C. W., Pullin, D. C., & Cusick, P. A. (1986). *Selling students short: Classroom bargains and academic reform in the American high school.* New York: Teachers College Press.

Senk, S. L., Beckman, C. E., & Thompson, D. R. (1997). Assessment and grading in high school mathematics classrooms. *Journal for Research in Mathematics Education, 28*(2), 187-215.

Sharan, S., Kussel, P., Hertz-Lazarowitz, R., Bejanaro, Y., Raviv, S., & Sharan, Y. (1984). *Cooperative learning in the classroom: Research in segregated schools.* Hillsdale, NJ: Lawrence Erlbaum.

Slavin, R. E. (1987). Ability grouping and student achievement in elementary schools: A best evidence synthesis. *Review of Educational Research, 57,* 293-336.

Slavin, R. E. (1990). Achievement effects of ability grouping in secondary schools: A best evidence synthesis. *Review of Educational Research, 60,* 471-499.

Smith, N. (1996). Standards mean business. In *Pre-Summit Briefing Materials: 1996 National Education Summit.* Palisades, NY: Governors' Commission Report for New Standards.

Smylie, M. A. (1996). From bureaucratic control to building human capital: The importance of teacher learning in education reform. *Educational Researcher, 25*(9), 9-11.

Solomon, P. G. (1995). *No small feat: Taking time for change.* Thousand Oaks, CA: Corwin.

Spady, W., & Marshall, K. (1990). *Vail leadership seminars.* Santa Cruz, CA: High Success Program.

Stedman, L. C. (1997). International achievement differences: An assessment of a new perspective. *Educational Researcher, 26*(3), 4-15.

Steffe, L. P., & D'Ambrosio, B. (1995). Toward a working model of constructivist teaching: A reaction to Simon. *Journal of Mathematics Teaching, 26*(2), 146-159.

Stein, M. K., Grover, B. W., & Henningsen, M. (1996). Building student capacity for mathematical thinking and reasoning: An analysis of mathematical tasks used in reform classrooms. *American Educational Research Journal, 33*(2), 455-488.

Steinberg, J. (1997, April 13). The classless classroom. *New York Times.* [On-line]. Available: www.nytimes.org.

Sternberg, R. J. (1985). *Understanding and increasing intelligence.* New York: Harcourt Brace.

Sternberg, R. J. (1988). *The triarchic mind.* New York: Viking.

Sternberg, R. J., Okagaki, L., & Jackson, A. S. (1990). Practical intelligence for success in school. *Educational Leadership, 48*(1), 35-39.

Stevenson, H. W., & Stigler, J. W. (1992). *The learning gap.* New York: Summit.

Stout, R. T. (1997). Staff development policy: Fuzzy choices in an imperfect market. *Education Policy Analysis Archives, 5*(4). [On-line]. Available: http://olam.ed.asu.edu.epaa/.

Strike, K. A. (1993). Professionalism, democracy, and discursive communities: Normative reflections on restructuring. *American Educational Research Journal, 30*(2), 255-275.

Strike, K. A. (1997). Centralized goal formation and systemic reform: Reflections on liberty, localism and pluralism. *Education Policy Analysis Archives, 5*(2). [On-line]. Available: http://olam.ed.asu.edu/epaa/.

Stumpf, T. (1995). A Colorado school's un-rocky road to trimesters. *Educational Leadership, 53*(3), 20-22.

Testa, D. (1996, March). Build on successes for reform that works. *NJEA Review*, p. 6.

Tobias, S. (1992, April). *Interest and metacognition in mathematics.* Paper presented to the American Educational Research Association, San Francisco.

Tobias, S. (1994). Interest, prior knowledge, and learning. *Review of Educational Research, 64*(1), 37-54.

Tobias, S. (1995). Interest and metacognitive word knowledge. *Journal of Educational Psychology, 87*(3), 399-405.

Tyler, R. W. (1949). *Basic principles of curriculum and instruction.* Chicago: University of Chicago Press.

Tyree, A. K. (1993). Examining the evidence: Have states reduced local control of curriculum? *Educational Evaluation and Policy Analysis, 15*(1), 34-50.

Tyson-Bernstein, H. (1988). The academy's contribution to the impoverishment of America's textbooks. *Kappan, 69*, 193-198.

U.S. Department of Education. (1991). *America 2000: An education strategy.* Washington, DC: Author.

U.S. Department of Education. (1997). *The national educational goals.* [On-line]. Available: www.ed.gov/pub/goals/summary.goals.html.

University of the State of New York. (1996). *Learning standards in math, science and technology.* Albany: Author. On-line at http://www.nysed.gov.

University of the State of New York. (1997). *Math, science and technology resource guide.* Albany: Author. [On-line]. Available: http://www.nysed.gov.

Unks, G. (1995). Three nations' curricula: Policy implications for U.S. curriculum reform. In A. C. Ornstein & L. S. Behar (Eds.), *Contemporary issues in curriculum* (pp. 415-429). Boston: Allyn & Bacon.

Urdan, T. C., & Maehr, M. L. (1995). Beyond a two goal theory of motivation and achievement: A case for social goals. *Review of Educational Research, 65*(3), 213-242.

Van Lehn, K. (1986). Arithmetic procedures are induced from examples. In J. Hiebert (Ed.), *Conceptual and procedural knowledge: The case of mathematics* (pp. 133-179). Hillsdale, NJ: Lawrence Erlbaum.

Vinovskis, M. A. (1996). An analysis of the concept and uses of systemic educational reform. *American Educational Research Journal, 33*(1), 53-85.

von Glasersfeld, E. (1990). Environment and communication. In L. P. Steffe & T. Wood (Eds.), *Transforming children's mathematics education: International perspectives* (pp. 30-38). Hillsdale, NJ: Lawrence Erlbaum.

Vygotsky, L. S. (1978). Mind in society: The development of higher psychological processes. In M. Cole et al. (Eds.), *Mind in society: The development of higher psychological processes.* Cambridge, MA: Harvard University Press.

Wallis, H. (Producer), & Rappen, I. (Director). (1942). *Now Voyager* [film]. Warner Brothers.

Wang, M. C., Haertel, G., & Walberg, H. (1993). Toward a knowledge base for school learning. *Review of Educational Research, 63*(3), 249-294.

Weinstein, R. S., Madison, S. M., & Kuklinsky, M. R. (1995). Raising expectations in schooling: Obstacles and opportunities. *American Educational Research Journal, 32*(1), 121-161.

Wells, A. S., Hirschberg, D., Lipton, M., & Oakes, J. (1995). Bounding the case within its context: A constructivist approach to studying detracking reform. *Educational Researcher, 24*(5), 18-24.

Wentzel, K. R. (1989). Adolescent classroom goals, standards for performance and academic achievement: An interactionist perspective. *Journal of Educational Psychology, 81*, 131-142.

Wentzel, K. R. (1993). Motivation and achievement in early adolescence: The role of multiple classroom goals. *Journal of Early Adolescence, 13*, 4-20.

Wertsch, J. V. (1979). From social interaction to higher psychological process: A clarification and application of Vygotsky's theory. *Human Development, 22*(1), 1-22.

Wiggins, G. (1989). Teaching to the authentic test. *Educational Leadership, 46*(7), 41-47.

Wiggins, G. (1995). Standards, not standardization: Evoking quality student work. In A. C. Ornstein & L. S. Behar (Eds.), *Contemporary issues in curriculum* (pp. 187-195). Boston: Allyn & Bacon.

Wiggins, G. (1996/1997). Practicing what we preach in authentic assessments. *Educational Leadership, 54*(4), 18-25.

Wisconsin Department of Public Instruction. (1996). *Position statement on standards.* Madison: Office of Public Accountability.

Zuckerman, M. (1996, September 16). Why schools need standards. In *U.S. News and World Report*, p. 128.

Index

**CORWIN
PRESS**

The Corwin Press logo—a raven striding across an open book—represents the happy union of courage and learning. We are a professional-level publisher of books and journals for K–12 educators, and we are committed to creating and providing resources that embody these qualities. Corwin's motto is "Success for All Learners."